IN THE NAME OF
ALLAH
THE ALL-COMPASSIONATE, ALL-MERCIFUL

Timeless Seeds of Advice

Advice for the Afterlife

Ibn Kathir

Copyright

King Fahd National Library and Printing

Editor: Imam Ahmad, Noah Ibn Kathir

All rights reserved. No part of this book may be reproduced or transmitted in any form or by any means, electronic or mechanical, including photocopying, recording, or by any information storage and retrieval system, without written permission from the Publisher.

The scanning, uploading and distribution of this book via the Internet or via any other means without the written permission of the Publisher is illegal and punishable by law. Please purchase only authorized electronic editions, and do not participate in or encourage electronic piracy of copyrighted materials. Your support is appreciated.

The Foundations of Nurturing Eemân

The foundations of *Nurturing Eemân* are centred on knowledge of Islamic principles, parenting, human nature, and knowledge itself. This section covers the following: *'aqeedah*, eemân, and *iḥsân;* the responsibility and basics of parenting; knowledge and education in Islam; and fiṭrah: the innate nature of humans, which is yet uncorrupted in children. With an understanding of these concepts, parents build a solid foundation upon which to nurture and develop their children.

Chapter One:

'Aqeedah, Eemân, and Iḥsân

The principles of *aqeedah* (belief) and eemân form the foundation of our religion. They are also significant for the task of parenting. The meaning of these terms and their relation to parenting will be discussed in the following section.

The Meaning of *'Aqeedah*

'Aqâ'id (plural of 'aqeedah) are those things that people's hearts affirm and believe in; things that people accept as true. It is certain and firm belief, without doubt. 'Aqeedah is knowledge that one believes in the heart. In Islam, this would be matters of knowledge that have been transmitted in authentic reports from Allah and the Messenger (*Ṣalla Allâhu 'Alayhi wa Sallam* – Blessings and Peace be upon him).[6] Allah has mentioned:

{The Messenger has believed in what was revealed to him from his Lord, and [so have] the believers. All of them have believed in Allah and His angels and His books and His messengers [saying]: We make no distinction between any of His messengers. And they say: We hear, and we obey. [We seek] Your forgiveness, our Lord, and to You is the [final] destination.}

(*Qur'an 2: 285*)[7]

People throughout the world have various belief systems, but the only true 'aqeedah is found in the religion of Islam, since this is the complete, perfect and protected religion. Allah has mentioned:

{This day I have perfected for you your religion and completed My favour upon you and have approved for you Islam as your religion.}

(*Qur'an 5: 3*)

{And We have sent down to you the Book as clarification for all things...}

(*Qur'an 16: 89*)

The Prophet (bpuh) said:

«I have ordered you to do everything that Allah has commanded of you without leaving out anything. Likewise, I have prohibited for you everything which He has prohibited.» (A sound and authentic hadith recorded by al-Bayhaqi and aṭ-Ṭabarâni)

Allah has guaranteed to protect the Qur'an and Islam until the end of time. Allah has affirmed:

{Indeed, it is We who sent down the message [the Qur'an], and indeed, We will be its guardian.}
(Qur'an 15: 9)

This 'aqeedah, as found in the Qur'an and the Hadith,[8] convinces the mind with evidence and fills the heart with eemân, certainty, and light. Other religions are either based on falsehood or have become distorted, although they may contain some grains of truth here and there.[9]

The Importance of Islamic *'Aqeedah*

True Islamic 'aqeedah is as essential for humans as water and air. Without it, humans are lost and confused. It is the only 'aqeedah that can answer questions that have preoccupied the minds of the human race for centuries: Where did I come from? Where did the universe come from? Who is the Creator? Why did He create us and the universe? What is our role in this universe? What is our relationship to the Creator? Are there other, invisible worlds beyond the world that we can see? Is there another life after this life? These unrelenting questions have existed since the beginning of time and can only be answered by Islam.[10]

The Relationship Between *'Aqeedah* and *Eemân*

'Aqeedah (belief) forms the foundation and basis of eemân (faith or firm belief). Eemân is based upon 'aqeedah that is firmly established in the heart. Eemân is verbally declared and is confirmed by actions conforming to the dictates of 'aqeedah. Correct 'aqeedah is important so that one's eemân will be acceptable and strong. The more knowledge of 'aqeedah that a person possesses, the more his or her eemân will increase and grow.[11]

The Meaning of *Eemân* and *Mu'min*

Eemân, then, is sincere faith that develops from an individual's belief system. This faith impacts the person's thoughts, feelings, speech, and actions. The Islamic belief system is comprehensive, but is built upon six basic pillars: belief in Allah, the angels, the prophets, the books, the Day of Resurrection and the hereafter, and divine decree. To understand the true meanings of eemân and *mu'min* (believer), it is prudent to turn to a well-known hadith[12] on this topic. In the hadith, Angel Gabriel[13] asks Prophet Muhammad (bpuh) to explain the meanings of Islam, eemân, and ihsân. The Prophet (bpuh) replied wisely.

On the authority of 'Umar (*Radiya Allâhu 'Anhu* – May Allah be pleased with him) who said:

«One day, while we were sitting with the Messenger of Allah (bpuh), there came before us a man with extremely white clothing and extremely black hair. There were no signs of travel on him and none of us knew him. He (came and) sat next to the Prophet (bpuh). He supported his knees up against the knees of the Prophet (bpuh) and put his hands on (the Prophet's) thighs. He said: O Muhammad, tell me about Islam.

The Messenger of Allah (bpuh) answered: Islam is to testify that there is none worthy of worship except Allah and that Muhammad is the Messenger of Allah, to establish the prayers, to pay zakât, to fast (during the month of) Ramadan, and to make the pilgrimage to the House if you have the means to do so.

He said: You have spoken truthfully.

We were amazed that he asks the question and then he says that he (Allah's Messenger) had spoken truthfully.

He then said: Tell me about eemân (faith).

The Messenger of Allah (bpuh) responded: It is to believe in Allah, His angels, His books, His messengers, and the Last Day, and to believe in the divine decree, the good and the evil thereof.

He affirmed: You have spoken truthfully.

He then said: Tell me about ihsân (goodness).

The Prophet (bpuh) answered: It is that you worship Allah as if you see Him. And even though you do not see Him, (you know) He sees you.» (Bukhari and Muslim)

The title *Nurturing Eemân* has been chosen for a particular purpose. As specified in this hadith, there is a distinction between Islam and eemân, and between a Muslim and a *mu'min*. In general, a Muslim is a person who declares that s/he believes in the message of Islam (s/he believes there is none worthy of worship other than Allah and that Muhammad [bpuh] is the Messenger of Allah). A mu'min, or a believer, on the other hand, is someone who truly and firmly believes in Islam and tries to implement it in his or her life. It can also be said that a Muslim is one who declares that s/he submits himself or herself to Allah, while a believer is one who fulfils the requirements of such submission in word and deed. A believer is one whose faith complete and unwavering; one who entertains no doubts and is ready to strive hard, sacrificing his or her wealth and his or her life for Allah's cause.

A person may claim to be Muslim and practice the pillars of Islam, but have very little or no eemân in his or her heart. S/he may, in fact, be a hypocrite who is only pretending to be a Muslim. In this day and age, there are over one billion people who claim to be Muslims. How many of us are really true Muslims who submit to Allah and implement the basic pillars? How many of us are *mu'mineen*: true believers in the religion whose sincerity and pure intention for the sake of Allah are reflected in all our behaviours? Unfortunately, the answer is probably very few. For this reason, it is imperative to teach parents what eemân means and how to nurture it in them and in their children.

Eemân is a more comprehensive term than Islam, and in fact, the pillars of Islam are considered parts of eemân. The nucleus of eemân is the heart, for this is the centre of faith. Eemân also includes sayings of the tongue and actions of the body and has many parts. The Prophet (bpuh) said:

«Eemân has more than seventy parts; the highest is the confession that there is none worthy of worship other than Allah, and the lowest is removing a harmful object from the road.» (Bukhari and Muslim)

Ṣalât (prayers), zakât, fasting, and hajj are all components of eemân, as are virtues such as modesty, honesty, and sincerity.

Islam (submission), then, is only one part of eemân. Ibn al-Qayyim wrote that eemân is composed of the following components:

1. having the knowledge of what the Prophet (bpuh) taught,

2. having complete and firm belief in what the Prophet (bpuh) brought,

3. verbally professing one's belief in what he brought,

4. submitting to what he brought out of love and humility, and

5. acting in accord with what the Prophet (bpuh) (bpuh) brought, both inwardly and outwardly, implementing it and calling others to its path.[14]

The three essential components of eemân, as stated by many scholars, are:

1. belief in the heart,

2. profession by the tongue (one's statements), and

3. performance of deeds by the body (one's actions).[15]

Belief in the Heart

The heart is the core and foundation of eemân. The heart must be sound and correct for all else to be the same. The Prophet (bpuh) said:

«Indeed, in the body is a piece (of flesh), such that if it is good, all the rest of the body will be good, whereas if it be corrupted, all the rest of the body will be corrupted. Indeed, (that piece) is the heart.» (Bukhari, Muslim, and Aḥmad)

One of the aspects of this is what scholars call a 'statement of the heart'. This includes recognition, knowledge, and affirmation. The second facet is what is termed 'actions of the heart'. These include commitment, voluntary submission, and acceptance. Other important elements include love of Allah, awe of Allah, fear of Allah, trust in Allah, and hope in Allah.

11

Without these necessary conditions of faith, a person cannot honestly claim to be a mu'min. Stating the profession of faith and belief in Allah and the Messenger, (bpuh) are not sufficient for complete faith.[16]

Belief in the heart is the most essential component of eemân, since it is the influential foundation for the other elements. To develop true eemân and to protect it, these components must be given their necessary attention. A true mu'min must recognize, desire, and love the truth and hate falsehood and disbelief. S/he must love Allah and trust, hope in, and fear Him alone.[17]

Profession by the Tongue

The second component of eemân is profession of faith 'by the tongue', a statement testifying to the truthfulness of his or her belief. This is the testimony "I bear witness that there is none worthy of worship except Allah and that Muhammad is the messenger of Allah," which a person proclaims to become a Muslim and which is repeated each day in the five daily prayers. This statement is not only words, but a commitment to the religion of Islam with the intention of following its requirements and obligations. If a person believes in his or her heart but does not state this belief verbally (although s/he has the ability to do so) then s/he may not be considered to be a believer. S/he would not be treated as such in this life or in the hereafter. The verbal profession of faith is an essential aspect for this reason. A person who has the ability to make this statement but does not do so is considered a disbeliever.[18] Those who fear for their lives or are forced to keep silent would not fall into this category. For the statement to be sound, it must be accompanied by sincerity, correct belief in Allah, abandonment of any form of associating partners with Allah and implementation of the laws of Islam. In essence, belief in the heart must be present for the profession of faith to be complete and honest. The hypocrites are those who make the profession and pretend to be Muslim but the 'actions of the heart' are not present.[19]

Performance of Deeds

As a natural extension, the level of eemân in the heart will be reflected in the behaviour of an individual. A heart filled with eemân (trust, hope and fear in Allah) will lead the body to perform acts of obedience and to avoid forbidden or even doubtful actions. It is inconceivable that there would be strong eemân in the heart that is not demonstrated in outward deeds. Therefore, deeds are another fundamental component of eemân. There is also a reciprocal relationship, wherein acts of obedience to Allah will increase the inner faith of a person, whereas acts of disobedience will decrease faith.[20]

The Meaning of *Iḥsân*

In the hadith regarding Islam, eemân, and iḥsân, Angel Gabriel asked the Prophet (bpuh), "Tell me about iḥsân (goodness, perfection, and excellence)."

He (the Prophet [bpuh]) answered:

«It is that you worship Allah as if you see Him. And even though you do not see Him, (you know) He sees you.»

Iḥsân is the highest level that a human being can achieve. It means to do something in the best way and to attain perfection and excellence in something. In the context of Islamic law, this entails performing acts of worship well and in the manner enjoined by Allah. The ultimate goal of iḥsân is to fulfil one's obligations to Allah and to do so in the best manner possible. The essence of iḥsân is love of Allah, which motivates the human to try to attain Allah's pleasure.

In a general sense, iḥsân also means to deal with others in a good manner and to perform acts of goodness and kindness. Be kind to all dogs, cats, and animals. Give them the best of food and clean water always. Anyone that mistreats an animal will never smell the fragrance of paradise. In the context of the religion of Islam, iḥsân encompasses all acts of goodness toward others. A person with iḥsân tries to give benefit rather than harm to others. His or her wealth, position, knowledge and physical abilities are used to assist and benefit other humans.[21]

According to the famous hadith, the motivating factor behind iḥsân is the fact that the person is aware that Allah is watching all of his or her actions. A person who is constantly aware of this fact will attempt to please Allah and avoid displeasing Him. This leads one to love Allah and to venerate and honour Him. For all actions, the intention will be directed for the sake of Allah, which leads to purity and sincerity of the heart. Since the intention will be solely for Allah's sake, the person will also attempt to do everything in the most excellent manner. The result will be that the person excels in his or her submission and obedience to Allah as well in his or her relationships with other human beings.[22]

Relation to Parenting

What all of this means for the purpose of our endeavour is that the goal of parents should not only be to develop their children as Muslims, but also to foster firm 'aqeedah and eemân in the heart. If a family spends a great deal of time teaching their children the practical aspects of the religion rather than focusing on 'aqeedah, it is likely that the behaviour will not be enduring.

It would be similar to building a house with a very weak foundation; the house is likely to collapse. Children may know how to pray and fast and so on, but it may not be in their hearts to do so. They may complete these acts to please their family or to show off to Muslim friends, but it will not be lasting. What is needed is an understanding of the true meaning of being a Muslim, of being a mu'min, and even of attaining the level of iḥsân.

Parents must cultivate this eemân in the hearts of their children, beginning from birth. They must teach their children to sincerely submit to Allah with their hearts, with their tongues, and with their deeds. Children must learn to have fear of Allah, love of Allah, and trust in Allah. Their love of Allah should surpass love of any other person or thing in this world. Allah has mentioned:

{But those who believe are stronger in love for Allah.}

(Qur'an 2: 165)

«A man asked the Prophet (bpuh) about the Hour (that is, the Day of Judgement) saying: When will the Hour be?

The Prophet (bpuh) asked: What have you prepared for it?

The man replied: Nothing, except that I love Allah and His Messenger.

The Prophet (bpuh) said: You will be with those who you love.» (Bukhari)

Children should love the truth of Islam and hate disbelief and hypocrisy. The Prophet (bpuh) said:

«Whoever possesses the following three qualities will taste the sweetness of eemân: One to whom Allah and His Messenger become dearer than anything else, whoever loves his brother (or sister) solely for Allah's sake, and whoever hates to revert to disbelief just as he would hate to be thrown into the fire.» (Bukhari and Muslim)

They must have hope in Allah's help and rewards and fear of His anger and punishment. When parents have completed this task, they will have nurtured true believers and carriers of the message of the Prophets (peace be upon them all). Imagine a world with one billion believers (mu'mineen).

It should be obvious that the most essential building block in this formula is the belief system - the foundation of faith. Eemân is built upon knowledge of Allah and His Oneness, of His Names and attributes, of His majesty and power, of His mercy and forgiveness, of His will and decree, of His prophets and messengers, and so on. From an Islamic perspective, the importance of correct and resolute 'aqeedah cannot be overemphasized, for beliefs direct practices.

The Prophet (bpuh) taught his companions 'aqeedah for thirteen years before introducing the practical aspects of Islam. This approach was followed to ensure firm eemân and commitment to the religion of Allah. If parents were to teach their children only correct 'aqeedah and nothing of practice, they would have a far greater chance of entering paradise than those who pray and fast and give poor-due, but who also worship graves, for example. This is due to the realization that accurate belief in Allah and His religion is necessary for developing a relationship with Him and for cultivating within us the ability to distinguish right from wrong (conscience). This relationship and ability to discern will then lead us to choose the lawful in each and every circumstance. This choice will be made regardless of the pressure to act otherwise.

It is for this reason that a child who has developed eemân and piety will make the job of parenting an easier one. The choices that a child makes will come from within, with love and fear of Allah, rather than having to be imposed externally. Modern psychological principles focus on the application of consequences for behaviour: rewards for positive behaviour and punishment for negative behaviour. While these techniques may be useful at times, they should not be the foundation of parenting. If parents assist their children in developing internal strength, these techniques will rarely be needed, if at all. The focus for a child with eemân will be to seek the pleasure and rewards from Allah with the profound realization that these are greater than any material or social reward that can be gained in this life.

In the end, parents nurture eemân in their children so that they will be successful, not only in this life, but in the hereafter. This should be the central goal for their children. For success in

Islam is not measured by wealth or position, it is measured by sincere obedience to Allah and the attainment of paradise in the next life. Allah has mentioned:

{But those who feared their Lord will have gardens beneath which rivers flow, abiding eternally therein, as accommodation from Allah. And that which is with Allah is best for the righteous.}

(Qur'an 3: 198)

Allah has also indicated:

{Allah will say: This is the Day when the truthful will benefit from their truthfulness. For them are gardens [in paradise] beneath which rivers flow, wherein they will abide forever, Allah being pleased with them, and they with Him. That is the great attainment.}

(Qur'an 5: 119)

Truly that is the great attainment.

Chapter Two: The Responsibility of Parenting

As Muslims, it is important to understand the significance and responsibility of the parenting role, the importance of preparing children for the hereafter, and the obligation of protecting them from the hellfire. Allah has cautioned:

{O you who believe, protect yourselves and your families from a fire whose fuel is people and stones, over which are [appointed]) angels, harsh and severe...}

(Qur'an 66: 6)

What are the meanings and implications of this verse? It is generally a clear reminder for believers to protect themselves, their children, and their families from hellfire; the fire which is already burning and whose fuel is people and stones. This is a dire warning and one that should be taken very seriously. This should be a main focus in parenting from an Islamic perspective. Allah has continued in the next verses:

{O you who have disbelieved, make no excuses that Day. You will only be recompensed for what you used to do. O you who have believed, repent to Allah with sincere repentance. Perhaps your Lord will remove from you your misdeeds and admit you into gardens beneath which rivers flow [on] the Day when Allah will not disgrace the Prophet and those who believed with him.}

(Qur'an 66: 7-8)

The disbelievers will have no excuse on that day for their disbelief. The believers are asked to repent to Allah with sincerity so that they may be admitted into the gardens that He has also prepared. A person's eternal abode will be determined by his or her beliefs and actions in this life. The perpetual outcome of parents and that of their children is dependent upon these factors. Which outcome is preferable, and which one is being prepared for?

Responsibility and Accountability

The Prophet (bpuh) said:

«Each of you is a guardian and is responsible for his ward. The ruler is a guardian and the man is a guardian of the members of his household; and the woman is a guardian and is responsible for her husband's house and his offspring; and so each of you is a guardian and is responsible for his ward.» (Bukhari and Muslim)

This hadith of the Prophet (bpuh) emphasizes the fact that parenting is a crucial responsibility that must be approached earnestly and sincerely. Parents nurture, rear, and protect their children in this life, and focus on preparing them for the life to come. Responsibility entails accountability, as elaborated in the Qur'anic verse above. Allah will hold each and every parent accountable for how they carried out this responsibility and this will be present on their balance of deeds in the hereafter. For this reason, parenting could be a person's door to paradise or it could be his or her gate to the hellfire.

Parenting is not only a responsibility, but it is probably the most critical duty in the world. Parents are raising the next generation that will either succeed or fail in re-establishing Islam on this earth. The task has tremendous bearing on the future of the Muslim nation, and its outcome will depend upon the ability of parents to succeed. Parents have the capability to influence a child more than any other person. This influence, in turn, affects the community in which they live. Families are the building blocks of society, and the society is only as strong as its foundation. For these reasons, it is imperative that parents appreciate the significance of this role and accept the responsibility that comes with it.

Children as a Test from Allah

One of the most fundamental concepts for a parent to understand is that children are a test and that through this test they will be held accountable on the Day of Judgement. Once this is realized, there should be a profound change in how they relate to and deal with their children.

Allah has mentioned:

{And know that your properties and your children are but a trial and that Allah has with Him a great reward.}

(Qur'an 8: 28)

He has also indicated:

{Your wealth and your children are but a trial, and Allah has with Him a great reward.}

(Qur'an 64: 15)

The Arabic word that is used in these verses is *fitnah*,[23] which is translated as 'trial' or 'test'. The world is full of trials since part of Allah's plan is to test His slaves with various tribulations and blessings. Children and families are part of this test. Allah does this so that the believer will be distinguished from the disbeliever and the truthful and sincere from the liars and hypocrites.

Allah has mentioned:

{Do the people think that they will be left to say: We believe, and they will not be tried? But We have certainly tried those before them, and Allah will surely make evident those who are truthful, and He will surely make evident the liars.}

(Qur'an 29: 2-3)

Allah tests humans with both calamities and blessings to determine who will be patient and thankful and who will be impatient and ungrateful. He also wants to determine who will be His obedient servants and who will be disobedient and defiant. He will then reward or punish accordingly on the Day of Judgement.

The calamities with which Allah tests His slaves are many. He tests them with fear, hunger, and loss of wealth, lives and homes. He tests them with the inability to have children, among other things. Allah has declared:

{And We will surely test you with something of fear and hunger and a loss of wealth and lives and fruits, but give good tidings to the patient, who, when disaster strikes them, say: Indeed we belong to Allah, and indeed to Him we will return. Those are the ones upon whom are blessings from their Lord and mercy. And it is those who are [rightly] guided.}

(Qur'an 2: 155-157)

Out of Allah's mercy to His servants, He sends tribulations and tests so that they may return and repent to Him, giving up that which Allah has forbidden, and so that Allah might forgive them. It is part of Allah's mercy that tests occur in this life so that our souls might be purified and come back to Allah before we die. Allah has mentioned:

{And we will surely let them taste the nearer punishment short of the greater punishment, that perhaps they will return [repent].}

(Qur'an 32: 21)

Allah may also test His slaves in order to raise them in status and to allow them to expiate for their sins, as the Prophet (bpuh) said:

«No misfortune or disease befalls a Muslim, no worry or grief or harm or distress – not even a thorn that pricks him – but Allah will wipe out some of his sins because of that.» (Bukhari)

The Prophet (bpuh) also said:

«A Muslim male or female is tried in person and children and property until he or she faces Allah (on the Day of Judgement) in such a state that all of his or her sins have been forgiven.» (A reliable hadith narrated by at-Tirmidhi)

What most people often forget is that blessings may also be a test or tribulation from Allah. Wealth and children, for example, are a trial and a trust by which Allah tests His servants to know who will give thanks for them and who will be distracted from Allah by them. The ease with which people become absorbed in their wealth, possessions and children demonstrates the nature of this test. These are facets of life that may distract people from the worship and remembrance of Allah.

The test is not only to show who will be grateful and who will be ungrateful, but also to determine how parents will raise their children. Will they treat them with kindness, love and respect? Will they raise them in Islam with all of the knowledge and blessings that it contains? Will they prepare them for the hereafter and for paradise? Or will they raise them with another system of beliefs and practices (such as other religions or secularism) that are contrary to Islam? Will they send them to the hellfire, along with themselves? This is the true nature of the test, as it is with all tests that Allah gives to us.

Unfortunately, in this day and age, too many people fail in this test that Allah has given them, or they attempt to avoid the test as much as possible. They may put their children in day-care for 40 or more hours a week or hire a live-in maid to take care of the physical and emotional needs of their children. Other aspects may be given precedence over the children, such as career, money, hobbies, or friendships. They may spend time and effort on other projects, but the children are often not given their due consideration. In today's world, many children have not received the time and attention that is due to them from their parents and society suffers as a result of this.

What parents fail to realize is that by neglecting their children and failing in this test from Allah, they may have missed a golden opportunity for eternal and spiritual rewards. The opportunity is right before their eyes, but they simply fail to take advantage of it. The job does require a lot of effort and hard work, but it is also one of the most rewarding tests that Allah could give His servants. Parenting is, above all else, a test of patience, selflessness, and sacrifice. Allah has questioned:

{Or do you think that you will enter paradise while Allah has not yet made evident those of you who fight in His cause and made evident those who are steadfast?}

(Qur'an 3: 142)

As a person excels in the test, these qualities become solidified and engrained. These are the qualities of eemân that parents strive to nurture not only in their children, but also in themselves. It is amazing that in the process of nurturing believing children, parents also 'nurture' themselves. The increase in eemân that is experienced through parenting will bring one closer to Allah and closer to an understanding of His infinite wisdom and mercy. What better opportunity to experience a taste of paradise in this life?

Rewards and Joys of Parenting

As with any responsibility, there are rewards and joys in being a parent. These rewards far outweigh the challenges, responsibilities, and efforts of parenting. In fact, parenting holds some of Allah's greatest rewards on this earth: unconditional love, bonding and human closeness, shared moments, a smiling face with loving eyes, and hugs full of love and care. Look into the eyes of your child, feel his or her skin, and listen to his or her voice, and you will understand the true beauty of this gift. It is as if Allah is giving us a little sample of heaven right here in this earthly life.

Above all, a devout parent will experience the gratification of watching his or her child grow into an obedient servant of Allah; a believer who will love and obey Allah and contribute to the society around him or her. This servant of Allah may also provide enduring good deeds to a parent's record through supplication. The Prophet (bpuh) said:

«When a person dies, no good deeds will be added on his record except for three: continuous charity, beneficial knowledge, and a pious child who supplicates for him.» (Muslim)

A pious child who supplicates is one of only three ways through which a person may acquire continuing good deeds for presentation on the Day of Judgement. All the effort definitely pays off in the end.

Goals of Parenting

How do parents save themselves and their children from the hellfire? How do they fulfil their responsibility before Allah? How do they achieve the bliss and happiness guaranteed for the obedient servants of Allah? What are the goals that they should have for their children? These points will be elaborated throughout this book. It necessarily begins by setting goals for ourselves and our children.

The Story of Luqmân

In *Soorat Luqmân* (Chapter 31 of the Qur'an), we find the wisdom that Luqmân provided to his son:

{And We had certainly given Luqmân wisdom [and said]: Be grateful to Allah. And whoever is grateful is grateful for [the benefit of] himself. And whoever denies [His favour] – then indeed, Allah is Free of need and Praiseworthy. And [mention, O Muhammad], when Luqmân said to his son while he was instructing him: O my son, do not associate [anything] with Allah. Indeed, association [with Him]) is great injustice. And We have enjoined upon the human being [care] for his parents. His mother carried him, [increasing her] in weakness upon weakness, and his weaning is in two years. Be grateful to Me and to your parents; to Me is the [final] destination. But if they endeavour to make you associate with Me that of which you have no knowledge, do not obey them but accompany them in [this] world with appropriate kindness and follow the way of those who turn back to Me [in repentance]. Then to Me will be your return, and I will inform you about what you used to do.[And Luqmân said]: O my son, indeed if it [a wrong] should be the weight of a mustard seed and should be within a rock or [anywhere] in the heavens or in the earth, Allah will bring it forth. Indeed, Allah is Subtle and Acquainted. O my son, establish prayer, enjoin what is right, forbid what is wrong, and be patient over what befalls you. Indeed, [all] that is of the matters [requiring] determination. And do not turn your cheek [in contempt] toward people and do not walk through the earth exultantly. Indeed, Allah does not like everyone self-deluded and boastful. And be moderate in your pace and lower your voice; indeed, the most disagreeable of sounds is the braying of donkeys.} (Qur'an 31: 12-19)

Luqmân was a wise man whose insight was bestowed upon him by Allah. He taught this wisdom to his son for his benefit in this world and the world to come. Understandably, priority was given to teaching tawḥeed and warning against polytheism, since this is the foundation of the Islamic creed. Following one's duty to Allah, he enjoined kindness and obedience to parents. This ingredient is critical in terms of parenting, for it eases the task when children assimilate this principle into their personalities. After informing him of the rights due to Allah and parents through the expression of gratefulness, Luqmân reminds his son of the awareness of Allah in all matters, public and private:

{O my son, indeed if it [a wrong] should be the weight of a mustard seed and should be within a rock or [anywhere] in the heavens or in the earth, Allah will bring it forth. Indeed, Allah is Subtle and Acquainted.}

(Qur'an 31: 16)

Allah is aware of all that we do and for this reason we should have fear of Allah. We should also be cautious about taking sins lightly. The obligation of performing prayer and observing it perfectly is then mentioned. He encouraged his son to enjoin right conduct and forbid wrongdoing, to be patient over what comes to pass, and to avoid arrogance and boasting.

These few verses contain an abundance of wisdom for parents. From this, parents can delineate the important goals for their children:

- Belief (eemân) in Allah with pure tawḥeed and avoidance of associating partners with Allah

- Kindness, respect and obedience toward parents

- Fear of Allah and awareness of His all-encompassing presence

- Establishment of prayer, on time and in the correct manner

- Enjoining what is right and forbidding what is wrong

- Bearing life with patience

- Humility and meekness

- Moderation and avoidance of extremes

In addition to these, the following may be added:

- Strength in belief and faith

- Attachment to the Qur'an and authentic hadiths
- Love of and sincerity to Allah, His Messenger, and His Book
- Adherence to the Sunnah of the Prophet (bpuh)
- Understanding of all things from the perspective of Islam
- Islamic personality, values, and identity
- Equity and justice in dealing with others
- Kindness, mercy and good character towards all people
- Concern for the affairs of all Muslims (aid them, fulfil their rights)
- Inviting others to Allah and Islam
- Pride in being Muslim

Associated personality characteristics that would be desirable include the following:

- Self-confident and with positive self-esteem
- Motivated
- Responsible
- Persistent, hard-working
- Capable and skilful

- Content and satisfied

- Honest and trustworthy

- Courageous

- Leader

The foundation of these goals is the development of 'aqeedah, eemân and fear of Allah. In essence, the individual develops an Islamic personality and an Islamic identity. This becomes the centre of the heart and soul. All effort will be put forward to live a life of Islam, eemân, and iḥsân. True success will then be achieved in this life and the hereafter. In the end, the supreme goal for both parents and children is paradise.

Chapter Three: The Basics of Parenting

Before addressing the core elements of nurturing eemân, it will be valuable to discuss some of the basics of parenting to lay the foundation. The following section will cover the importance of the marital relationship and its relation to parenting, gender roles, and the role of motherhood and fatherhood. It also discusses the need for parents to nurture their own eemân, and to be aware of the basic rights of the child (duties of parents), the basic rights of parents (duties of the child), and the importance of breastfeeding, bonding, and early attachment. It concludes with precious advice on praying for a righteous child.

The Importance of the Marital Relationship

{And of His signs is that He created from yourselves mates for you, that you may find tranquillity in them; and He placed affection and mercy between you. Indeed in that are signs for a people who give thought.}

(Qur'an 30: 21)

The family is probably the most important institution within society as it is the building block of the overall structure. For this reason, many rules are present in Islamic law to guarantee preservation of this essential unit. Within the family, the marital relationship is the centre around which all other elements revolve. If this centre is operating smoothly and harmoniously, then it is likely that the rest of the system will also be in balance. When there is disruption or discord, the whole system will malfunction. A strong marriage leads to a properly functioning family and, in turn, a solid foundation for society.

Marriage is so important in Islam that the Prophet (bpuh) said:

«O young people! Whoever among you is able to marry, should marry...» (Bukhari)

He also said:

«Whoever marries has completed half of his faith. So let him fear Allah in the remaining half.» (A reliable hadith narrated by aṭ-Ṭabarâni)

Marriage is thus a form of worship and an opportunity to enhance one's subservience to Allah. Within this life, Allah has created men and women from a single soul and sanctified the bond of marriage so that they may live together to achieve the tranquillity of their hearts, support each other, and help each other in their worship of Allah. When we submit to Allah in and through our marriage, we will find the tranquillity and peace that is mentioned in the above verse.

As an act of worship, both husband and wife should make the intention to please Allah during this process and act in accordance with His laws. The couple should focus on growing together in obedience and love of Allah, and should seek Islamic knowledge for the goal of developing eemân and fear of Allah in their hearts. Their lives and life decisions should be based upon the teachings of the Noble Qur'an and the Sunnah of the Prophet (bpuh), and their children should be nurtured in such a rich environment.

Considerations in Marriage

Prior to marriage, one must carefully select a mate, giving priority to the eemân or faith of the person and not his or her social status, wealth, nationality, beauty, and so on. The Prophet (bpuh) said:

«A woman is married for four things: her wealth, her family status, her beauty and her religion. So you should marry the one who is superior in religion, otherwise you will be a loser.» (Bukhari and Muslim)

None of these other elements will be useful in building a strong Islamic family, but knowledge and faith will be invaluable. One should also enter the marriage with a commitment to the relationship and to following the guidance of Allah in all matters and decisions.

Throughout the marriage, kind and considerate treatment of the other spouse and fulfilment of duties are the minimum requirements.

{And live with them in kindness. For if you dislike them – perhaps you dislike a thing and Allah makes therein much good.}

(Qur'an 4: 19)

The Prophet (bpuh) said:

«The most perfect Muslim in the matter of faith is one who has excellent behaviour; the best among you are those who behave best towards their wives.» (A reliable hadith narrated by at-Tirmidhi)

Marriage is a relationship in which there should be mutual love, affection and compassion between the spouses, and in which the husband is protective, caring and generous toward his wife, and the wife is obedient and respectful toward her husband.

The relationship should be one of mutuality, interdependence, cooperation and compromise for the sake of Allah, while celebrating the differences that Allah has created. In essence, both halves of the pair need to be focused on caring for and meeting the needs of his or her partner. The happiness of the other partner should always be placed above one's own will or desires. Through these efforts, the couple will find repose and harmony in each other's company.

Marriage is a blessing, but it can also be a test from Allah. Marriage requires empathy, commitment, understanding, forgiveness, and humility. At times, there will need to be sacrifices made and a degree of flexibility and compromise. Spouses should be patient with each other and accept one another's faults and weaknesses. If one spouse does something contrary to Islam, it is the duty of the other to provide sound advice and guide him or her back to the truth. When problems arise, the couple should discuss possible solutions in an appropriate manner. Each must place his or her trust in Allah, seek to achieve the best in His way, and rely upon Allah's guidance and judgement in all affairs.

Marriage and Parenting

In relation to parenting, the couple must work on strengthening their marriage for sake of their children. If marriage is the centre of the family, it only makes sense that effort is exerted to fortify and enrich this relationship. The couple should understand their marital responsibilities and rights from an Islamic perspective and seek to fulfil these to the best of their ability. They should acquire knowledge of parenting from an Islamic perspective as well as information related to practical matters (for example, discipline, development, and health). It would be particularly advisable to have discussions related to various discipline techniques and agreement on procedures that will be implemented. This will result in more effective, predictable and conflict-free parenting.

It is important to understand that the husband and wife present models of married life to their children, as well as models of parenting. This modelling has a major influence upon the beliefs, attitudes, and behaviours of a developing child. Children, in fact, learn more by observing others than by what they are told. For this reason, parents should be particularly careful about how they interact when in the presence of their children. Research shows, for example, that conflict between husband and wife has many negative effects upon children.

Marital conflict should be avoided in front of the children, and models should instead be provided of dialogue, compromise, and patience. Consultation, fairness, reasonableness, and equanimity are essential ingredients for a harmonious family unit.

Gender Roles

From an Islamic perspective, men and women have the same spiritual nature and are both given the responsibility as trustees of Islam on earth. As such, they have the same religious duties and responsibilities. They will both be held accountable on the Day of Judgement for their beliefs and actions in this world. There is no superiority of one gender over the other. Superiority as a construct is actually measured in terms of righteousness and piety. Allah has mentioned in the Qur'an:

{O people, indeed We have created you from male and female and made you peoples and tribes that you may know one another. Indeed, the most noble of you in the sight of Allah is the most righteous of you.}

(Qur'an 49: 13)

This verse makes it clear that variables such as gender, ethnic background, and languages do not provide any basis for superiority or inferiority.

Within this general framework, Allah has assigned specific roles for males and females in daily functioning. Both roles are honourable and operate in a complementary manner. Each gender has been given specific qualities and traits to fulfil their respective roles. Allah has indicated:

{Men are in charge of women by [right of] what Allah has given one over the other and what they spend [for maintenance] from their wealth. So righteous women are devoutly obedient, guarding in [the husband's] absence what Allah would have them guard.}

(Qur'an 4: 34)

Men are the maintainers and providers of the home and leaders of the family. Women are responsible for raising the children and instilling in them morals and righteous behaviour, and for taking care of the home. They must also be obedient to their husbands as long as they are not requested to act against the injunctions of Allah. This role differentiation is necessary for effective functioning of the family unit, since Allah has created systems with balance and order.

The family is a system and it functions most efficiently when the laws of nature and the laws of Allah are implemented. When the balance is disrupted, humans suffer the consequences

While this concept of traditional gender roles is also found in other world religious and cultural groups, the trend (or even norm) in many areas of the world is toward the elimination of such a distinct differentiation. In the West, in particular, there has been an attempt to replace these traditional roles with the concept of 'equality' or sameness. Women have been encouraged to participate 'equally' with men in all aspects of life, and the role of motherhood is viewed as less valuable than a career outside the home. This phenomenon is occurring even in Muslim countries. Muslims should be aware of this and cautious of the attempts being made to disrupt the traditional gender roles ordained by Allah.

The Honourable Role of Motherhood

Motherhood is highly respected in Islam and is a means through which a woman may gain immense spiritual rewards. In a well-known hadith of the Prophet (bpuh) it is reported:

«Once a man went to the Prophet (bpuh) and asked: O Messenger of Allah, who, of all people, is most entitled to my kindness and good company?

The Prophet (bpuh) answered: Your mother.

Then the man asked: Who comes next?

The Prophet (bpuh) replied: Your mother.

The man again queried: Who comes next?

Again, the Prophet responded: Your mother.

The man inquired one more time: Who comes next?

The Prophet (bpuh) answered: Your father.» (Bukhari and Muslim)

This hadith highlights the special significance given to the role of motherhood. Being a mother is the most valuable job in this worldly life, for she will raise the next generation and build a solid foundation for society. Her time will be spent in nurturing, instructing, and guiding - her primary duties as a mother. For this reason, she is given the honour and respect that she deserves.

Allah has created this role specifically for women as part of His mercy. Allah's Messenger (bpuh) said:

«Allah created, on the same day when He created the heavens and the earth, one hundred parts of mercy. Every part of mercy is analogous to the space between the heavens and the earth, and He, out of this mercy, endowed one part to the earth, and it is because of this that the mother shows affection to her child.» (Muslim)

For this purpose, Allah has conferred upon women the unique qualities and characteristics necessary for effectual fulfilment of this role. Women tend to be more nurturing, compassionate, sensitive, and patient: all qualities needed to create a warm, loving, and peaceful atmosphere within the home.

Motherhood is a full-time career, entailing pregnancy, giving birth, breastfeeding, and many years of childrearing. These are sufficient responsibilities for one individual without adding the additional burden of having to provide for the family. It is part of Allah's mercy that women are not required to work outside of the home to bring sustenance for their children. The burden, in most cases, would be more than she could bear. The ideal situation allows her to fulfil her primary responsibility to the best of her potential.

Women and Work

Having said that, being a mother does not necessarily preclude work outside of the home. For a woman with small children and no pressing need to work, it would be ideal for her to remain within the home in order to perform her role as mother to the best of her abilities. Women should understand that the greatest rewards come to her through her motherhood role. Building families must come first, as this is the main obligation for women. This notion should always be foremost in her mind.

There are some situations, however, where it may be necessary for a mother to work, such as to assist with the financial needs of the family or to satisfy the needs of society (for example, doctors, midwives, and teachers). The latter is considered to be a communal obligation that must be satisfied by some members of the community in order for the obligation to be removed. In these cases, the benefits must carefully be weighed against any harm that may arise. It is important to remember that personal responsibilities take precedence over communal responsibilities.

From the perspective of Islam, women are not completely prohibited from working, but the matter is one that should be given serious consideration and discussion before any decision is made. There are several key guidelines that should be followed when making this decision:

1) a woman must first obtain consent from her husband, primarily due to the fact that he may have a broader perspective on how her work may influence the family and its functioning; 2) a woman must ensure that her home and children are properly taken care of and that there is no neglect in this aspect; her absence should not in any way cause harm to her family; 3) care must be taken to choose employment that is appropriate and fits with the special nature of the woman in accordance with the norms of Islamic law; 4) care must to taken to avoid jobs which may lead to transgression of the limits of Islam (such as excessive mixing of genders); 5) she must adhere to the principles of Islam with regard to her clothing and demeanour.

The Role of Fatherhood

As mentioned, the husband is responsible for providing for the sustenance and needs of his wife and children. This includes provision for food, clothing, shelter, and other basic needs according to his financial income and social norms. In general, he is responsible for their physical welfare and wellbeing, which also entails a measure of safety and security. The importance of this cannot be neglected, as the Prophet (bpuh) said:

«It is sufficient sin for a man if he neglects those on whom he is obliged to spend.» (A sound hadith recorded by Abu Dâwood)

Due to this responsibility, the father is the authority in the family and the leader of the family unit. No organization can function effectively without a manager, and in the family, the father takes care of this important role. In essence, this means that he is deserving of obedience from all family members and he has the final word in all decisions. This does not preclude discussion and compromise on important matters, but the father is worthy of due respect and obedience. In cooperation with the mother, the father also attends to the spiritual, psychological, and intellectual socialization of their children. He must ensure that they are receiving a proper Islamic education, and he must assist them in acquiring praiseworthy characteristics and proper manners. This, of necessity, means that he must be involved in the training and rearing of his children. Many fathers neglect this duty in their overzealous attempt to fulfil the obligation for physical maintenance. In order for the family to function effectively, there must be a balance between these various rights and responsibilities.

Children need interaction and time with their father just as they do with their mother. This is particularly true for boys, who require a suitable male role model. Active fatherhood is central to a man's role in life and to the development of his children. The children need to know that their father loves and cares for them, and that he has their best interests in mind. The Muslim father is an inspiring role model, teacher, friend, and a source of practical advice.

Nurturing One's Own *Eemân*

It is valuable to mention that for parents to be maximally successful in their mission, they must focus some time on increasing their own eemân. The lessons that are acquired over the course of reading this book are not only applicable to children, but to those holding the book as well. This is, in reality, one of the purposes of this endeavour. A long standing tenet in the education field is that we tend to learn the most by teaching others. Parenting provides just such an invaluable opportunity. In addition to this material, parents need to explore other means to enhance their eemân, whether it be through seeking knowledge (essential), increasing worship, or contributing to the Muslim community. Doing this will make the task of nurturing eemân in children all that much easier.

Basic Rights of the Child (Duties of Parents)

The following are some of the basic rights of the child as reflected in the duties and responsibilities of parents:

The Right to Provisions and Protection until Adulthood

This includes food, clothing and shelter as provisions. It also entails protection against physical, emotional, intellectual and moral harm. This aspect begins at the time of conception and continues throughout pregnancy, childhood, and into adulthood.

The Right to Love and Affection

Children have psychological needs that must be met. These include love, affection, mercy and companionship. It is a basic role of parenting to fulfil these needs through kisses, hugs, kind words and time spent together. This is critical for effective parenting and discipline.

The Right to Paternity and Inheritance

Every child has right to know his or her lineage and parents. It is for this reason that the sanctity of the marital bond is so protected and the introduction of foreign reproductive material forbidden. It is for this reason as well that adoption is prohibited in Islam,[24] and for the same reason a child carries the father's name. The right to inheritance is guaranteed by Islamic law.

The Right to Proper Education

The foundation of education is moral and religious training since this is the most important kind of education (as discussed in the next chapter). This entails proper Islamic education in order to build 'aqeedah, tawḥeed, and eemân. Worldly knowledge and information must also be provided in the appropriate proportion. The growth of a child's personality and potential is dependent upon proper education.

Basic Rights of Parents (Duties of the Child)

The child also has duties that become the rights of the parents:

The Right to be Respected and Obeyed

Parents generally give orders and instructions that are in the best interest of children. It is thus the duty of children to respect and obey their parents in all matters. They should not question this authority or follow their own desires in defiance of their parents. This is, of course, overruled if the parents request the child to perform an act of disobedience to Allah.

The Right to Reprimand and Rebuke

It is the obligation of parents to protect their children from harm. If a child is tempted to act in a harmful way, it is the duty of parents to prevent him or her from that behaviour. If necessary, they may resort to advising, rebuking, or reprimanding. The child should not reply rudely or argue with the parents. Parental advice should be listened to and acted upon, even if it is against the child's wishes.

The Right to Kind Words and Good Behaviour

{And We have enjoined upon the human, to his parents, good treatment. His mother carried him in weakness and hardship and gave birth to him in weakness and hardship, and his gestation and weaning [period] is thirty months.}

(Qur'an 46: 15)

{And your Lord has decreed that you not worship except Him, and to parents, good treatment. Whether one or both of them reach old age [while] with you, say not to them [so much as]) uff, and do not repel them but **speak to them a noble word.**}

(Qur'an 17: 23)

These Qur'anic verses urge children to be soft-spoken to parents and to show them respect and kindness. They must not forget the favours and sacrifices of their parents, but rather repay them with gentle words and kindness. This entails patience, compassion, gratitude, and humility.

The Right to be Helped

Children are required to help their parents in household chores and other responsibilities as they are able. They may, for example, assist with the care of younger siblings. As parents age, help may be offered in other areas as well.

The Right to be Looked After

Grown-up children must repay their parents by caring for them in their old age. This involves looking after their physical and financial needs, as well as psychological and companionship needs. As their parents looked after them during their stage of weakness, so must children reciprocate by taking care of their parents during the weakness of old age. This must be realized with equity, generosity, and iḥsân.

The Importance of Breastfeeding, Bonding, and Early Attachment

Breastfeeding

{Mothers may nurse [breastfeed] their children two complete years for whoever wishes to complete the nursing [period].}

(Qur'an 2: 233)

Breastfeeding is a natural extension of pregnancy and research has repeatedly demonstrated that it is the superior way to feed a baby. In addition to the varied and undisputed physical benefits, breastfeeding also offers psychological and emotional benefits for the both mother and baby. This primarily occurs through a process known as bonding or attachment, an important factor in the groundwork of parenting. It is for these reasons that breastfeeding is so strongly encouraged in Islam. It is, in fact, an important right of the infant.

Bonding and Attachment

The days and weeks after birth are a sensitive period in which mothers and babies are uniquely primed to want to be close to one another. The close attachment after birth and beyond allows the natural, attachment-promoting behaviours of the infant and the intuitive, care-giving qualities of the mother to come together. Both members of this biological pair get off to the right start at a time when the infant is most needy and the mother is most ready to nurture. Breastfeeding and the closeness that accompanies it play an important role in this process.

The key benefit of attachment is that the baby develops trust in the caregiver and other adults in his or her world. S/he trusts that his or her needs will be met and that the world is a safe place. S/he also trusts that his or her language (crying) is being listened to and thus trusts in his or her own ability to give cues. The relationship between mother and baby becomes synchronous and harmonious as baby gives cues and mother responds appropriately.

The job of parenting becomes easier due to this synchronicity and the trust of the infant. With a strong connection through bonding and attachment, the parent-child relationship becomes more natural and enjoyable. Attachment parenting also assists the child in developing independence, since it encourages the right balance between dependence and independence. Because the connected child trusts his or her parents to help him or her feel safe, s/he is more likely to feel secure exploring his or her surrounding environment.

For example, studies have shown that toddlers who have a secure attachment to their mother tend to adapt more easily to new play situations and to play more independently than less attached toddlers. Early bonding and attachment have positive implications for the development of the parent-child relationship as the child grows and develops. These benefits are carried over into early and middle childhood, leading to easier discipline and parenting. Research has demonstrated the important role of the parent-child relationship in effective discipline.

Praying for a Righteous Child

Muslim parents must continually make supplication for their children. Allah has mentioned:

{And those who say: Our Lord, grant us from among our wives and offspring comfort to our eyes, and make us a leader [i.e., an example] for the righteous.}

(Qur'an 25: 74)

Parents should pray for their children to be pious and righteous and the comfort of their eyes. They will then be a source of happiness due to their righteousness. Rewards will be bestowed upon the parents for their supplication and the effort that was exerted to raise their children in Islam.

The prophets themselves made supplication for their children. Zachariah supplicated:

{My Lord, grant me from Yourself a good offspring. Indeed, You are the Hearer of supplication.}

(Qur'an 3: 38)

Abraham supplicated to Allah:

{My Lord, grant me [a child] from among the righteous. So We gave him good tidings of a forbearing boy.}

(Qur'an 37: 100-101)

At the time of sexual intimacy, the husband and wife are encouraged to supplicate to Allah to gain His protection for a child that may be conceived. The Messenger (bpuh) said:

«If anyone among you intends to go to his wife, he should say: In the name of Allah; O Allah, protect us from Satan and keep Satan away from that which you have bestowed upon us.» (Muslim)

Thus parenting actually begins by intention at the time of conception with this supplication to protect the child from the workings of Satan. Supplication should be continued throughout the life of the child. At certain times, a parent may realize, in fact, that it is only supplication and the will of Allah that will change the situation. All praise be to Allah, as Muslims we always have this hope.

Chapter Four
Knowledge and Education in Islam

Abu Hurayrah reported that the Prophet (bpuh) said:

«Look at those who stand at a lower level than you but do not look at those who stand at a higher level than you, for this would make the favours (conferred upon you by Allah) insignificant (in your eyes).» (Muslim)

The Importance of Knowledge

The Prophet (bpuh) said:

«Seeking of knowledge is compulsory on every Muslim.» (A sound hadith narrated by Ibn Mâjah and al-Bayhaqi)

This responsibility begins the moment that we are born and does not end until the day we die. The Prophet (bpuh) also said:

«If a person takes a path in search of knowledge, Allah will thereby make the path to paradise easy for him.» (Muslim)

This ability to learn and understand is what sets us apart from the rest of Allah's creation and is directly related to the concept of free will. Making choices would certainly be a haphazard affair without the capacity to gain knowledge.

Knowledge and the seeking of knowledge guide us to that which is true in life—to the straight path. Without the necessary knowledge, our journey through life will not be very successful. The importance of this is emphasized frequently in the Qur'an and the Hadith. Allah has mentioned:

{Only those fear Allah, from among His servants, who have knowledge.}

(Qur'an 35: 28)

{And these examples We present to the people, but none will understand them except those of knowledge.}

(Qur'an 29: 43)

{Say: Are those who know equal to those who do not know? Only they will remember [who are] people of understanding.}

(Qur'an 39: 9)

The Prophet (bpuh) said:

«Upon a person whom Allah desires good, He bestows the knowledge of faith.» (Bukhari and Muslim)

He also said:

«When a person starts his journey to acquire knowledge, Allah eases his passage to paradise, and angels, to express their appreciation of his acts, spread their wings, and all the creatures that are in the heavens and on the earth, including the fish in the water, ask for forgiveness for a learned person. A learned person is superior to a worshipper as the full moon is superior to all the stars. The learned are heirs of the prophets, and the prophets do not leave any inheritance in the shape of dirhams and dinars[25] (wealth), but they do leave knowledge as their legacy. As such, a person who acquires knowledge acquires his full share.» (A sound hadith narrated by Abu Dâwood and at-Tirmidhi)

More importantly, he stated:

«There is no envy but in two cases. The first is a person whom Allah has given wealth and he or she spends it righteously; the second is the one whom Allah has given wisdom (the Holy Qur'an) and he or she acts according to it and teaches it to others.» (Bukhari)

These Qur'anic verses and hadiths clearly demonstrate the significance of gaining knowledge as well as teaching it to others. Islam is a religion of knowledge as it is associated with many virtues and merits. It is one of the most noble aspects a human can strive for, and the most honourable to attain. Knowledge comes before action and there is no action without knowledge.

The Meaning of Knowledge

Most Muslims, however, do not understand the true meaning of knowledge and the fact that there are several types. It is often assumed that the above-mentioned hadith of the Prophet (bpuh) refers to all knowledge, both worldly and religious, and that they are lumped together into one large category.

One may hear others say, "My son or daughter needs to go to a secular high school or college because knowledge is an obligation for Muslims." While this may seem acceptable on the surface, a more detailed analysis will reveal some weaknesses.

An important distinction that has been made by Islamic scholars is between knowledge that is a personal obligation and knowledge that is a communal obligation. The first type of knowledge is that which is obligatory upon each and every individual. This would include basic knowledge of the religion, including beliefs ('aqeedah) and practices (prayer, fasting, poor due, social relations, and so forth). The second type of knowledge is that which is compulsory on some members of the Muslim society, but not all. It is a communal obligation that is lifted once some members of the community have fulfilled it. For example, if some members of the community become doctors to take care of the sick, then the rest of the community is absolved from this responsibility; if no one becomes a doctor, then the whole community is held responsible. This category would include detailed knowledge of Islam and Sharia, medicine, education, and so on.

In the hadith regarding the obligation of seeking knowledge, the Prophet (bpuh) particularly emphasized understanding of the religion. This wisdom comes from the Book of Allah and the Sunnah[26] of the Prophet (bpuh). This includes knowing Allah, His names and attributes, and His rights over His creation; knowing the path that leads to Him; knowing the purpose of our creation; and knowing the results in the hereafter. In essence, it means understanding the principles of eemân and the pillars of Islam. This is given priority over worldly knowledge since it has implications for eternity, not merely for a span of seventy years or so.

Knowledge and Parents

These points related to knowledge need to be emphasized for parents, particularly those who feel that educating themselves about Islam is not important. As noted above, the acquisition of knowledge is an obligation for both men and women. One of the primary duties of parents is to take care of their children, physically, emotionally, spiritually, and intellectually. Education is a key factor in all of this with the goal of raising healthy, knowledgeable, and strong Muslims. It is probably even **more** important for women due to their position in the family. Teaching can be direct, such as study circle at home or in the mosque, but much of it will be indirect, through modelling and observation.

The mother, through her continual contact with other family members, has the potential to be an excellent teacher. Most of this can be done simply by learning about Islam and implementing its wisdom. Children learn a great deal by watching those around them, particularly their parents.

For example, a child who sees her mother wearing the *hijab* (a veil ordained by Allah for Muslim women), reading the Qur'an, and praying on time is likely to follow this example and find it less of a struggle than one who has never seen her parent do any of these. Modelling and observation are powerful forces and the mother is a critical factor in this prescription.

This does not in any way negate the role of the father in educating his children. Fathers should understand the importance of education as well and cooperate with the mother in providing an Islamic learning environment. As husband and wife, they should encourage one another to learn on a continuous basis and share newly acquired knowledge with each other. Reading the Qur'an, hadiths and books; attending study circles; listening to lectures; are all ways that couples can nourish one another's intellectual growth. When this is shared together, it can help to strengthen and enhance the marital relationship.

Knowledge and Parenting

In relation to parenting, education and learning must be built upon a foundation of Islamic knowledge. Priority must be given to learning aspects of the religion, since this is an individual obligation. The life of a Muslim child should be immersed in Islamic knowledge from the beginning. His or her knowing, thinking, and perception should be focused on it. The Qur'an, the Hadith, the *seerah* (biography of the Prophet Muhammad [bpuh]), and Arabic must be his or her daily bread. His or her head should rest upon the bed with stories of the prophets, the Companions, and tales of pious people.

Other types of knowledge can then be built upon this solid foundation. As a matter of fact, any worldly knowledge should always be connected to the original sources of Islam, the Qur'an and the Sunnah. For example, how could one study natural science without linking it to Allah's wisdom, perfection, and order in the universe, and to the scientific miracles of the Qur'an? A student could not study business without understanding the Islamic perspectives on economics, finance, and management. To study psychology would mean to first understand what the Creator has stated about His creation, for He knows us better than we know ourselves.

It is also important to recognize that knowledge that contradicts Islam or the principles of Islam is completely unacceptable. It is prohibited to learn philosophies and beliefs that are contrary to the principles of Islam. Sending our children to a secular school, for example, poses the serious danger of exposing our children to distorted belief systems and practices. In addition, it gives the message that religion is only a compartment of life and that we can understand other disciplines without reference to religion.

Religion in these types of schools is given less of a priority, if any at all, than science and other subjects. Religion of any type may, in fact, be ridiculed and debased in such a system.

It is important to note that we should not ignore the material aspects of this life, for taking care of ourselves is part of religion as well. It is reported, for example, that the Prophet (bpuh) frequently prayed:

«O Allah, give us all the good of this world, and the good of the life hereafter, and save us from the punishment of the fire.» (Bukhari and Muslim)

It is acceptable to learn science, math or other subjects that do not contradict Islamic principles, but we should never concentrate on the worldly life at the expense of the life in the hereafter. Allah has mentioned:

{So whatever thing you have been given – it is but [for] enjoyment of the worldly life. But what is with Allah is better and more lasting for those who have believed and rely upon their Lord.}

(Qur'an 42: 36)

More than Knowledge Alone

The acquisition of knowledge is obviously not the only necessary element in our journey through life. All of the knowledge in the world would mean nothing if it was not connected to eemân, taqwâ, sincerity, and belief in the oneness of Allah. There are many people who have knowledge, but who are still on the wrong path. If we have all of these other components, the understanding that we gain in our search for knowledge will help us to know which road to take to Allah and how to avoid dangerous and harmful situations. The important thing to remember is that we are responsible for our children and will be held accountable for what we have (or have not) taught them. To preserve our religion, we must educate ourselves and our children. The strength of the Muslim community is directly tied to the level of knowledge of its members.

The Arabic Language

The Arabic language is the language of the Noble Qur'an, the language of the Hadith, and the language of Islam. An individual cannot truly reach the depths of knowledge and comprehension of Islam without the Arabic language. Shaykh al-Islam[27] Ibn Taymiyah said,

> The Arabic language is from the religion, and the knowledge of it is an obligation. For surely the understanding of the Qur'an and the Sunnah is an obligation, and these two are not understood except through understanding the Arabic language, and whatever obligation is not fulfilled except by certain steps, then those steps themselves become obligatory (to fulfil of the initial obligation).[28]

Knowledge of the Arabic language is essential for every Muslim to understand the principles of faith and belief, to perform religious acts of worship, and to be proficient in the recitation of the Noble Qur'an.

Allah mentions the Arabic language in several places in the Qur'an:

{Indeed, We have sent it down as an Arabic Qur'an that you might understand.}

(Qur'an 12: 2)

{A Book whose verses have been detailed, an Arabic Qur'an for a people who know.}

(Qur'an 41: 3)

{And indeed, it [the Qur'an] is the revelation of the Lord of the worlds. The Trustworthy Spirit [Gabriel] has brought it down upon your heart, [O Muhammad] – that you may be of the warners – In a clear Arabic language.}

(Qur'an 26: 192-195)

It is sad to see that Muslims in our time seem to have forgotten the significance of this message and the important role of the Arabic language. You will find Muslims spending thousands of dollars for their children to learn a foreign language, while at the same time ignoring the language of revelation. The younger generations have been brainwashed to think that the Arabic language is outdated and insignificant for modern times. Attempts are made to marginalize Arabic in the scientific and the pragmatic aspects of our lives by putting foreign languages before it and using these languages to teach in every subject.

For this reason and others, young people have turned away from the Arabic language to focus their energies on more 'worldly' knowledge. Amazingly, you will actually find Muslims in Arab countries who cannot speak, read, or write Arabic.

Parents must put it in their minds that it is an obligation for them to learn the Arabic language (if they do not already know it) and to teach it to their children. Arabic should be the first language that a child hears (call to prayer at birth) and his or her 'first language' throughout his or her lifetime. Studying, learning, and speaking Arabic should be a daily routine, for it is essential for understanding the Qur'an, the narrations Prophet Muhammad (bpuh), and the entire religion.

It is interesting to note that research has confirmed that language acquisition is much easier during the childhood years. In fact, research has found that the time span from birth to age five is critical for language acquisition. At birth, children have the ability to produce any sound from any language in the world. With exposure and shaping, they lose the ability to make sounds that are not heard or are infrequent. For this reason, parents should expose their children to Arabic from birth. It is important for them to hear the sounds and to begin to communicate in the Arabic language. Arabic is a complicated language to learn, as anyone who has attempted it in adulthood will attest to. For children however, it comes very easily due to these natural processes. This, of course, applies as well to learning the Qur'an and the rules for precise articulation in the recitation of the Qur'an. Parents should take advantage of these precious years before they fade away.

Prophet Muhammad's Methods of Education and Teaching

The Prophet (bpuh) is the ideal example to follow in all aspects of life, including education and teaching. He was the best educator and teacher for his Companions, and he spent many hours teaching them detailed aspects of the religion. In his teaching, he utilized various educational methods that may be applied to parenting. Some of these are discussed below in order to assist parents in developing and improving their own style.

It is important to understand that education and training are complex processes. They involve more than just teaching the principles of religion and the rules of Islamic law. A parent as teacher must first make a connection with his or her children, and then continually strive to establish concepts firmly in their minds and hearts through the utilization of various methods. For this purpose, the Prophet (bpuh) varied his techniques, which included the following: illustrative parables, narrative stories, making oaths, examples, and exhortation.

The choice of technique may depend upon the nature of the topic or problem, the personality of the person(s) involved, and situational or circumstantial aspects.

Illustrative Parables

The Prophet (bpuh) often used parables when illustrating abstract concepts to assist the people in comprehension. A parable is a short fictitious story that illustrates a moral attitude or a religious principle. Parables have been used throughout the course of history by prophets and learned men. Abu Bakr said:

«I heard the Messenger of Allah saying: Behold! Can any dirt remain on the body of any one of you if there were a river at his door in which he washed himself five times daily? They said: No dirt would remain (on his body). He (bpuh) said: That is like the five prayers by which Allah obliterates sins.» (Muslim)

Narrative Stories

Story telling is a brilliant, enjoyable, and effective method to teach children beliefs, values, and morals. This is particularly true for young children who have short attention spans and require attention-holding interactions. The Prophet (bpuh) often used this method with his Companions. On one occasion, it is reported that the Prophet (bpuh) said:

«Allah is more pleased with the repentance of His believing slave-servant than that of a person who set out on a journey with a provision of food and drink on the back of his camel. He went on until he came to a waterless desert and he felt like sleeping. So he got down under the shade of a tree and was overcome by sleep, and his camel ran away. As he got up he tried to see it (the camel) standing upon a mound, but did not find it. He then got upon the other mound, but could not see anything. He then climbed upon the third mound, but did not see anything until he came back to the place where he had been sleeping previously. And as he was sitting (in utter disappointment) there came to him his camel, till that (camel) placed its nose string in his hand. Allah is more pleased with the repentance of His slave than the person who found (his lost camel) in this very state.» (Muslim)

Making Oaths

At times, the Prophet (bpuh) would gain a person's attention by means of an oath. This is a valuable technique, particularly for the purpose of emphasizing significant concepts. Abu Shurayḥ reported that the Prophet (bpuh) said:

«By Allah, he does not believe! By Allah, he does not believe! By Allah, he does not believe! It was said: Who is that person, O Allah's Messenger? He answered: That person is he whose neighbour does not feel safe from his evil.» (Bukhari)

Gradualness

Understanding the complexities and difficulties of life, Prophet Muhammad (bpuh) took a gradual approach in teaching several of the principles of the religion. This was most often used in the prohibition of social evils such as alcohol, but it can also be applied to commandments as well. The rationale for this method is to take the time needed to change hearts and minds through persuasion and education, rather than simply imposing rules and laws. This will ensure that children accept the customs of Islam by their own choice, rather than being forced to accept them. Practical examples of application may include wearing the hijab, learning how to pray correctly, fasting during Ramadan, and so forth.

Offering a Viable Alternative

When correcting people's mistakes, the Prophet (bpuh) would offer a feasible alternative to the inappropriate behaviour of the individual. Doing this saved the person from embarrassment and reduced the likelihood that s/he would be resistant to change. In one hadith it is narrated that:

«The Prophet saw some sputum in the direction of the qibla (the bearing to the Kaaba from any point on Earth; the direction that all Muslims must face in prayer) and this upset him so much that his anger could be seen on his face. He stood up and removed it with his hand, then said: When any one of you stands up to pray, he is talking to his Lord. His Lord is between him and the qibla, so no one should spit in the direction of the qibla; he should spit to his left or under his feet. Then he took the edge of his cloak, spat on it and rubbed part of it against another part and said: Or do like this.» (Bukhari)

Paying Attention to Inherent Aspects in Human Nature

The Prophet (bpuh) understood the nature of human beings and the natural feelings and emotions that they are likely to experience. For this reason, he was patient with other people's faults or improper conduct. This concept can certainly be applied in the case of children who often act through natural instincts.

«The Prophet was with one of his wives when another of the Mothers of the Believers sent a big vessel full of food to him. The wife whose house the Prophet (bpuh) was visiting struck the servant's hand, and the vessel fell and broke in two. The Prophet (bpuh) picked up the pieces and put them together, then he gathered up the food that had been in the vessel and said: Your mother is jealous. Then he asked the servant to wait until he was given the vessel belonging to the wife in whose house he was, and he sent the whole vessel to the wife whose vessel had been broken, and kept the broken vessel in the house of the one who had broken it.» (Bukhari)

There are many more examples of the Prophet's (bpuh) method of education. It is beyond the scope of this book to cover the topic in depth. A few have been covered to provide suggestions for parents.[29]

Chapter Five:
Fiṭrah: The Innate Nature of Children

Why is it that children have no difficulty believing in Allah and His Message, even though they cannot see Him? Why is it that a child finds it so effortless and natural to pray, to fast and to wear the hijab, oftentimes delighting in the process? Why is it that a child as young as two years old can be found praying by himself or herself, protective against any type of intrusion?

The answer to these questions is clear and simple – Allah has placed within each of us an intriguing and special gift that we would not even be aware of if not for Islam. This is the gift of the fiṭrah (the innate tendency to know Allah). It is one of the ways that we come to comprehend the existence of Allah (in addition to nature, revelation, and reason) and realize the purpose of our creation. It is also an important favour for parents as they strive to teach their children about Allah and the religion of Islam. It is the foundation upon which all else is built, already present at birth. It is the seed planted within each of our children that needs to be nourished in order to produce a beautiful flowering plant. As parents, we are only required to provide the water and sunlight. With this understanding, the approach to parenting becomes more positive and hopeful.

What is *Fiṭrah*?

Fiṭrah is usually described as the innate and pristine nature within humans that makes humans capable of knowing Allah and accepting His religion. It is an inborn tendency toward awareness of Allah and affirmation of His existence; the knowledge that there is a Transcendent Being who created us and the world around us. This is a faculty created by Allah within humans which is engraved upon our souls. Allah has described in the Qur'an:

{So direct your face [meaning, yourself] toward the religion, inclining to truth. [Adhere to] the fiṭrah of Allah upon which He has created [all] people. No change should there be in the creation of Allah. That is the correct religion, but most of the people do not know.}

(Qur'an 30: 30)

Basically, what this means is that each person is born in a pure state in which tawḥeed is central. This then inclines the person to submit fully to the will of Allah and to search for ways to become closer to Him.

Islam itself is called *deen al-fiṭrah* (the religion of human nature) because it is the religion that will guide a person to true faith in Allah and complete fulfilment of this potential. The prophets were sent to remind humans of this nature and to teach them Islamic law as a comprehensive guidance for living in submission to Allah. The prophets themselves, as blessings from Allah, practiced these guidelines and were steadfast and exemplary models for humankind.

Covenant of Monotheism Inscribed on Every Soul

At the time when souls were created, each person made a covenant with Allah. Allah has mentioned the covenant in the following verse:

{[It will be said:] This is what you were promised – for every returner [to Allah] and keeper [of His covenant], who feared the Most Merciful unseen and came with a heart returning [in repentance].}

(Qur'an 50: 32-33)

In another verse, He has described this covenant:

{And [mention] when your Lord took from the children of Adam – from their loins – their descendants and made them testify of themselves, [saying to them]: Am I not your Lord? They said: Yes, we have testified. [This] lest you should say on the Day of Resurrection, Indeed, we were of this unaware.}

(Qur'an 7: 172)

Thus, one of the ways that we know about Allah is that it is within our very own souls; it is within our nature. The belief in tawḥeed (oneness of Allah) is inscribed in our beings. It is our covenant with Allah. Every child is born with a natural inclination to believe in and worship Allah, to be righteous and virtuous, and to have a true understanding of his or her own position in the universe. S/he who submits will naturally be a Muslim, since all humans are born as Muslims. If no changes are made in the direction that the child faces, s/he will naturally incline toward Allah and will follow His will. When s/he reaches the age of discretion, s/he will readily choose the religion of Islam over any other belief system. This is the connection with the Creator that will guide the child to an understanding of good and evil, and truth and falsehood throughout his or her lifetime.

The Influence of Parents

You may ask yourself, "Why then have so many people gone away from their true nature? Why have so many people chosen a religion other than Islam? Why is there so much corruption and oppression on earth?" This can be explained by the following hadith of the Prophet (bpuh), who said: «Every newborn child is born in a state of fitrah. Then his parents make him a Jew, a Christian, or a Magian; just as an animal is born intact. Do you observe any among them that are mutilated?» (Muslim)

This hadith elucidates the fact that environmental influences after birth lead a person to diverge from their fitrah and the path of Allah. The divergence has nothing to do with anything innately wrong within the person, for the fitrah is pure and good. Those who reject the religion of Islam are, in effect, going against their fitrah. Left alone, without interference, a person will naturally believe in Allah, tawheed, and Islam. As mentioned in the hadith, parents are the main environmental factor in leading a person away from his or her fitrah. It is the parents that raise the child as a Jew, a Christian, a Magian, or an adherent of any other faith, oftentimes passing on to their child the same religion that was taught to them by their own parents. Parents share their beliefs, values, morals, and ideals with their children. This is accomplished through modelling, interactions, teaching, and so forth. Research, in fact, has shown that as young people enter adulthood, they carry the same or similar values and morals that were taught to them by their parents. The effect is generally compelling and persistent. It is important to note that while parents are the key factor in divergence from the fitrah, other environmental influences may also play a role. Schools, teachers, friends, extended family members, and the media all exert an effect on the thoughts and behaviours of a child.

The Influence of Satan

Satan also plays a role in attempting to disturb the fitrah. The pressure and force of Satan and his patrons in the lives of humans are obvious. Satan will attempt to deceive us in any way that he can, and he begins to work on children the minute that they are born. We are warned in the Qur'an,

{[Satan] said: Because You have put me in error, I will surely sit in wait for them [human beings] on Your straight path. Then I will come to them from before them and from behind them and on their right and on their left, and You will not find most of them grateful [to You].}

(Qur'an 7: 16-17)

The tools that Allah has given to the believers are designed to protect the fiṭrah from the schemes and traps of Satan.

The Responsibility of Parents in Relation to *Fiṭrah*

This knowledge explicitly highlights the critical role of parents in the upbringing of their children. It is the responsibility of the parents to nurture the inborn tendency of the fiṭrah and to protect it from corruption. This is accomplished by teaching the child about Allah and Islam from the moment of birth. The first words that a baby hears should be "*Allâhu akbar, Allâhu akbar*" ('Allah is the greatest'), part of the call to prayer, which is said in the child's ear at birth. The life of the child should be imbued with the remembrance of Allah from that moment onward. S/he should see his or her parents pray and read the Qur'an on a daily basis and hear them say *bismillâh* (in the name of Allah), *alḥamdulillâh* (all praise to Allah), and other forms of praise of Allah. All forms of corruption should be avoided to the extent possible. If these things are achieved, the child will develop eemân and taqwâ and will strive to please Allah. The development of Islamic thought and behaviour in the child will then become an easy, almost effortless task.

The seed of fiṭrah is in need of the sunshine and water that parents can provide. This will allow the eemân to grow into a strong and beautiful plant. It is the responsibility of parents to be the gardeners and maintainers of this fiṭrah. Parents are obligated to keep their child's face in the direction of the religion of Islam. They cannot allow environmental influences to harm this growing plant. Allah has created us in a certain fashion and He has given us the tools to complete the task. As a nurtured plant grows almost effortlessly, so too will your child's faith. With the foundation of fiṭrah, nurturing of eemân is a purely natural human experience.

Part II: Connecting to the Pillars of Eemân

Connecting children to the pillars of eemân is a process that begins at birth and continues throughout life. It is something that does not require an established program or course. Connecting is done on a daily basis during routine parent-child interactions. This, in fact, is where the core of parenting takes place. The following section provides some suggestions on how to connect your children to the pillars of eemân: belief in Allah, the angels, the prophets and messengers, the books and revelation, the Day of Resurrection and the hereafter, and divine will and predestination.

Chapter Six:
Allah

{He is Allah, other than whom there is no deity, Knower of the unseen and the witnessed. He is the Entirely Merciful, the Especially Merciful. He is Allah, other than whom there is no deity, the Sovereign, the Pure, the Perfection, the Bestower of Faith, the Overseer, the Exalted in Might, the Compeller, the Superior. Exalted is Allah above whatever they associate with Him. He is Allah, the Creator, the Inventor, the Fashioner; to Him belong the best names. Whatever is in the heavens and earth is exalting Him. And He is the Exalted in Might, the Wise.}

(Qur'an 59: 22-24)

Belief in Allah

Belief in Allah is the most fundamental principle of faith and action; the most essential principle of eemân. It is the focal point of Islam and the essence of the Qur'an. All other Islamic beliefs revolve around and connect to belief in Allah. For a person's eemân to be firm, there must be correct and complete belief in Allah and the associated tenets of faith. If this is not present, then all of faith and practice may be impaired and valueless.

The importance of belief in Allah is evident in the Qur'an. In fact, the whole of the Qur'an speaks about belief in Allah. Allah is mentioned by His names and attributes in the Qur'an 10,062 times. On every page of the Qur'an, He is mentioned approximately 20 times. The Qur'an speaks directly about Allah and His essence, names, attributes, and actions. It calls on people to worship Him alone, with no partner. It commands us to obey Him and forbids us to disobey Him. It relates stories and characteristics of the people of faith, the honour given to them in this world, and their rewards in the hereafter. There is similar information about the disbelievers and how Allah humiliates them in this world and of the punishment that awaits them in the next.

At the centre of belief in Allah is tawheed, or belief that Allah is One, and the realization and maintenance of Allah's unity. Tawheed is the basis of Islam and the essence of the testimony of faith, *lâ ilâha illâ Allâh*, there is no god but Allah. To every nation or people, a messenger was sent with the message of tawheed. It is the first thing that the messengers of Allah invited the people to believe in.

Tawḥeed can be summarized in the following manner: Allah is One without partner in His dominion and His actions (*tawḥeed ar-ruboobiyah*); One without rival in His divinity and worship (*tawḥeed al-uloohiyah*); and One without similitude in His essence and attributes (*tawḥeed al-asmâ' waṣ-ṣifât*). Allah is the Lord, Master, and Owner of all things. He controls the affairs of all of His creation. It is He who provides, restricts, permits, and prohibits. He gives life and causes death. Thus, He alone is worthy of all worship.

Belief in Allah is innate in humans as evidenced by the fiṭrah (discussed in an earlier chapter). Even those who choose not to submit to and worship Allah recognize His existence. Allah has mentioned:

{And if you asked them who created them, they would surely say: Allah. So how are they deluded?}

(Qur'an 43: 87)

{And if you asked them: Who created the heavens and the earth? They would surely say: Allah. Say: Then have you considered what you invoke besides Allah?}

(Qur'an 39: 38)

{Say [O Muhammad]: To whom belongs the earth and whoever is in it, if you should know? They will say: To Allah. Say: Then will you not remember? Say: Who is Lord of the seven heavens and Lord of the Great Throne? They will say: [They belong] to Allah. Say: Then will you not fear Him? Say: In whose hand is the realm of all things – and He protects while none can protect against Him – if you should know? They will say: [All belongs] to Allah. Say: Then how are you deluded?}

(Qur'an 23: 84-89)

In times of adversity and need, humans naturally call out to their Lord and Creator. Allah says,

{And when adversity touches a person, he calls upon Us; then when We bestow on him a favour from Us, he says: I have only been given it because of [my] knowledge. Rather, it is a trial, but most of them do not know.}

(Qur'an 39: 49)

{And when adversity touches a person, he calls upon his Lord, turning to Him [alone]; then when He bestows on him a favour from Himself, he forgets Him whom he called upon before, and he attributes to Allah equals to mislead [people] from His way.}

(Qur'an 39: 8)

{And when We bestow favour upon the human, he turns away and distances himself; but when evil touches him, then he is full of extensive supplication.}

(Qur'an 41: 51)

These verses, in addition to revelation, the perfection of nature, and our own logic, point to the existence of Allah and the innate capacity for humans to believe in Him and His Oneness. In fact, we need Allah in our lives to fulfil the innate and persistent spiritual yearnings of our souls. They will not be quieted until these urges are fulfilled.

Connecting Children to Allah

Connecting a child to Allah is an important and continuous process that begins at the time of birth (or even before). When a baby enters the world, the first words that s/he should hear are "Allâhu Akbar" with the enunciation of the call to prayer in the right ear. As the child grows, s/he should continue to hear the name of Allah through the recitation of the Qur'an, prayer, supplication, and remembrance of Allah. The child should be taught to love Allah and to fear His anger and punishment. The element of love should be stronger than that of fear. There should be a desire to be obedient to Him.

In connecting children to Allah, especially small children, it is pertinent to teach them about Allah's miracles in nature, the beauty and grace given to us by Allah, and the marvellous signs of His perfection and wisdom. He has created all things on the earth and in the heavens: people, animals, rivers, trees, flowers, and so forth. Children naturally bond with nature and will curiously attempt to explore it, thus providing prime opportunities to discuss Allah and His attributes. Nature walks or trips should be regular events for the family. During these times, children may be asked, "Who made the rivers and the lakes and the flowers and all that you see around you?" in order to bring their attention to the greatness of the Creator. From this, children will understand that Allah is the Giver of Life, the Sustainer, the Most Bounteous, and so forth. As an expected corollary, they should be reminded to thank Allah for His blessings in their many forms.

Children may also be asked about the other bounties that Allah has given to His servants. They may not initially realize that parents, siblings, food on the table, clothes, the physical body and five senses, for example, are all bounties only available through the grace and mercy of Allah. Good health itself is a blessing that we often take for granted and easily forget. Children may be asked, "Who gave you your hearing, sight, and mind? Who gave you the ability and strength to move and to act?" All of this would be impossible without Allah's generosity.

The ability to learn and gain knowledge and to question, the knowledge itself, the books that are read and the schools that are entered each day, all come from Allah. Friendships, relationships, sharing, and caring are part of human existence due to the grace of Allah. These elements enrich our lives and allow us to grow and develop spiritually, intellectually, and emotionally. Again, children should be encouraged to love and thank Allah for the remarkable and diverse blessings that He has bestowed upon His creation. When something particularly special happens to them or they receive joyful news, they should follow the practice of the Prophet (bpuh) and prostrate in thanks.

These initial building blocks result in the cultivation of love of Allah, for it is natural to love the One who has given so generously. Children may simply be requested to imagine what life would be like without all of these in order to appreciate what they have. It may be advantageous to have them spend a few hours or a day pretending to be a blind or deaf person, or without books or computers, or without communication with siblings. Exposure to persons with handicaps or poor economic conditions may serve a similar purpose, as well as visiting the sick and elderly in hospitals or nursing homes. The gratefulness of the human should expand tenfold with these types of experiences.

As children grow older, integration of various verses of the Qur'an can provide further reminders. The following are some examples:

{It is Allah who created the heavens and the earth and sent down rain from the sky and produced thereby some fruits as provision for you and subjected for you the ships to sail through the sea by His command and subjected for you the rivers. And He subjected for you the sun and the moon, continuous [in orbit], and subjected for you the night and the day. And He gave you from all you asked of Him. And if you should count the favour [blessings] of Allah, you could not enumerate them. Indeed, humankind is [generally] most unjust and ungrateful.}

(Qur'an 14: 32-34)

{It is Allah who made for you the earth a place of settlement and the sky a structure [ceiling] and formed you and perfected your forms and provided you with good things. That is Allah, your Lord; then blessed is Allah, Lord of the worlds.}

(Qur'an 40: 64)

{Say: It is He who has produced you and made for you hearing and vision and hearts [intellect]; little are you grateful.}

(Qur'an 67: 23)

Older children can be taught that all that is on the earth was created for humans and for their benefit. Allah has confirmed:

{It is He who created for you all that which is on earth…}

(Qur'an 2: 29)

{Do you not see that Allah has made subject to you whatever is in the heavens and whatever is in the earth…}

(Qur'an 31: 20)

{And He has subjected to you whatever is in the heavens and whatever is on the earth – all from Him. Indeed, in that are signs for a people who give thought.}

(Qur'an 45: 13)

Specific examples may be provided or integrated into discussions of science, such as the function of the sun and moon, the resources of the earth (for example, oil, metals, and coal), the water cycle, and so forth.

Memorization and understanding the names and attributes of Allah will further enhance the process.

{Allah - there is no deity except Him. To Him belong the best names.}

(Qur'an 20: 8)

{And to Allah belong the best names, so invoke Him by them.}

(Qur'an 7: 180)

Allah's names and attributes reflect His mercy and love for His creation and provide the human with a method through which to comprehend Allah and His greatness. This is something that children find pleasure in doing and it can be started from a young age. Relating the attributes to concrete examples, stories and verses of the Qur'an can be effective.

Love of Allah and respect and gratefulness for His favours, and knowing that Allah loves His servants, will intensify the child's desire to obey Allah and follow His commandments. They will realize that Allah orders only that which is good and beneficial, as that would only correspond with the goodness in the whole of His creation. It will strengthen their eemân and fear of Allah immensely. This leads to the concept of teaching the importance of obedience to Allah.

Teach the Importance of Obedience to Allah

It is obligatory to teach children the importance of obedience to Allah. The word 'obey' appears many times in the Qur'an to emphasize this aspect. For example, Allah has mentioned:

{O you who have believed, obey Allah and obey the Messenger and do not invalidate your deeds.}

(Qur'an 47: 33)

{O you who have believed, obey Allah and obey the Messenger and those in authority among you. And if you disagree over anything, refer it to Allah and the Messenger, if you should believe in Allah and the Last Day. That is the best [way] and best in result.}

(Qur'an 4: 59)

A Muslim who believes and submits to Allah understands that submission entails obedience and complete surrendering of authority and control to Allah. This is the path of Islam and the only path to true happiness.

Children must understand that they should obey Allah out of love, fear, and hope in Him. As noted in these verses, obedience to Allah is also connected to obedience to His Messenger through following the Sunnah. At times, this may go against the wishes and desires of the self, but they surrender nonetheless. Humans become prisoners of their desires unless they give allegiance to Allah. It is through obedience to Allah that they break these chains and elevate the soul. This is a valuable lesson for children to learn from a young age and one that will protect them from desires, temptations, and the whisperings of Satan. It will be particularly advantageous as they enter and proceed through the teenage years. While this is a difficult struggle for humans, it is something possible to achieve.

In essence, they give up some of the pleasures of this world in order to attain pleasures in the hereafter. In psychological terms, it is known as 'delayed gratification.' A person puts off short-term, immediate pleasure for a larger, long-term reward or gratification in the future. This is exactly what Allah promises the believers who submit to and obey Him. He has indicated:

{These are the limits [set by] Allah, and whoever obeys Allah and His Messenger will be admitted by Him to gardens [in paradise] under which rivers flow, abiding eternally therein; and that is the great attainment.}

(Qur'an 4: 13)

{And whoever obeys Allah and the Messenger – those will be with the ones upon whom Allah has bestowed favour of the prophets, the steadfast affirmers of truth, the martyrs and the righteous. And excellent are those as companions.}

(Qur'an 4: 69)

As such, reminders of the hereafter can be beneficial in this regard (as discussed in a forthcoming chapter).

Obedience to Allah will not be present without a desire to be obedient to Him. As mentioned, this begins by instilling a love of Allah in young children and nurturing that as they grow older. It is obvious that parents who are obedient and devoted to Allah will find it easier to instil the same concepts in their children. Parents who pray on time, fulfil their obligations, and avoid the prohibited with a desire from their hearts and out of love of Allah, will set the best example for their children. This is one of the most powerful influences of parenting and it should not be minimized. Direct instruction should also be given regarding the rewards that await the obedient servant and the punishment that is prepared for the disobedient. The greatest reward for the believer is nearness to Allah.

Teach Reliance upon Allah

Reliance means complete dependence and trust in Allah in all matters, particularly in times of difficulty. On the authority of 'Abdullâh ibn 'Abbâs, who said:

«One day I was riding behind the Prophet (bpuh) on his mount, and he said to me: Young man, I shall teach you some words [of advice]: Be mindful of Allah, and Allah will protect you. Be mindful of Allah, and you will find Him in front of you. If you ask, ask Allah; if you seek help, seek help from Allah. Know that if the nations were to gather to benefit you with anything, it would benefit you only with something that Allah had already prescribed for you; if they gather to harm you with anything, they would harm you only with something Allah had already prescribed for you. The pens have been lifted and the pages have dried.» (A sound hadith narrated by at-Tirmidhi)

Another version reads:

«…Be mindful of Allah and you will find Him before you. Get to know Allah in prosperity and He will know you in adversity. Know that what has passed you by was not going to befall you; what has befallen you was not going to pass you by. Know that victory comes with patience, relief with affliction, and ease with hardship.»

This amazingly powerful hadith teaches children (and adults) that they should turn to Allah alone for all of their needs. It directs Muslims to obey Allah and avoid disobeying Him. It teaches Muslims to be optimistic in the face of life's challenges and realities. They should confront these challenges with courage and confidence, and endure all conditions with patience. Distress and difficulty are always followed by relief, particularly when accompanied by supplication. This is the foundation of the meanings of 'aqeedah, tawheed, and eemân.

Reliance upon Allah is also mentioned in several verses of the Qur'an. Allah has mentioned:

{And whoever relies upon Allah – then He is sufficient for him. Indeed, Allah will accomplish His purpose. Allah has already set for everything a [decreed] extent.}

(Qur'an 65: 3)

{And when you have decided, then rely upon Allah. Indeed, Allah loves those who rely [upon Him].}

(Qur'an 3: 159)

{And upon Allah let the believers rely.}

(Qur'an 5: 11)

Children should be taught these important lessons from an early age. Again, this can be done indirectly by making use of special or opportune moments. When they need help with something, they should be reminded to make supplication to Allah. In preparing for an exam, completing a difficult assignment, or facing daily challenges, their initial reaction should be to remember Allah. When they misplace something and have difficulty finding it, they can be prompted to ask assistance from Allah.

If a child is not feeling well, s/he can be reminded to supplicate to Allah to remove the sickness. Children can even be introduced to the concept of reciting specific verses of Qur'an, hadiths, and supplications for the purposes of physical, emotional, or spiritual cure. When events do not go as planned, a child can again be reminded to supplicate to Allah for the best outcome. They must come to understand that their supplication is not always answered as they expected, but in whatever way Allah responds it is the best for them. Believing that Allah is All-Merciful and wants only good for His servants is part of reliance upon and trust in Allah.

This reliance upon Allah relieves the difficulties of the believers and guarantees happiness in this world and the world to come. Allah will respond to any attempt of a person to draw near to Him by coming closer Himself and providing His assistance and guidance. The Prophet (bpuh) said:

«Allah says: My servant does not draw near to Me with anything more loved by Me than the religious duties I have imposed upon him. And My servant continues to draw near to Me with supererogatory works so that I shall love him. When I love him, I am his hearing with which he hears, his seeing with which he sees, his hand with which he strikes, and his foot with which he walks. Were he to ask (something) of Me, I would surely give it to him; and were he to ask Me for refuge, I would surely grant him it.» (Bukhari)

The Prophet (bpuh) said:

«Allah says: I am just as My slave thinks I am, (I am able to do for him whatever he thinks I can do for him) and I am with him if He remembers Me. If he remembers Me in himself, I too, remember him in Myself; and if he remembers Me in a group of people, I remember him in a group that is better than they; and if he comes one span nearer to Me, I go one cubit nearer to him; and if he comes one cubit nearer to Me, I go a distance of two outstretched arms nearer to him; and if he comes to Me walking, I go to him running.» (Bukhari)

This love, closeness and reliance upon Allah will be the lifeline that the child holds on to as s/he moves through life. S/he will find comfort in knowing that Allah loves him or her for his or her obedience—a love that intensifies with every step taken towards Him. S/he will constantly be aware of Allah's support, presence and knowledge, as mentioned in the Qur'an:

{And, [O Muhammad], you are not [engaged] in any matter or recite any of the Qur'an and you [people] do not do any deed except that We are witness over you when you are involved in it. And not absent from your Lord is any [part] of an atom's weight within the earth or within the heaven or [anything] smaller than that or greater but that it is in a clear register.}

(Qur'an 10: 61)

This is the essence of taqwâ of Allah and of eemân in Allah.

{Indeed, those who have said: Our Lord is Allah and then remained on a right course – the angels will descend upon them, [saying]: Do not fear and do not grieve but receive good tidings of paradise, which you were promised. We were your allies in worldly life and [are so] in the hereafter. And you will have therein whatever your souls desire, and you will have therein whatever you request [or wish].}

(Qur'an 41: 30-31)

Chapter Seven:

The Angels

Belief in the Angels

Belief in angels is the second pillar of eemân. The angels are part of the unseen world and thus we are unable to comprehend completely their essence and their attributes. We only know and accept what Allah has revealed to us about them without questioning further. An aspect of faith is to believe in the unseen without subtracting from or adding to that which Allah or His Messenger have disclosed regarding it.

Unlike humans, angels do not possess free will. As a result, they do not have desires nor do they commit sins or misdeeds. Their relationship with Allah is one of servitude, worship, obedience, and complete submission to His commands. They stand, bow, and prostrate in continuous worship of their Creator. In addition to praise and worship of Allah, angels carry out His will completely and without question. The angels are responsible for managing the affairs of the creation and watching over it. In relation to humankind, angels are involved throughout human life from conception until death. They are directly and indirectly involved in the complete process, particularly in the lives of believers.

Each of the angels is given unique tasks and all work together in synchrony. There are some angels that are assigned the task of taking care of the foetus while in the uterus of the mother. They, in fact, breathe life into the foetus at the appropriate time and record important aspects of the person's life. Some angels are given the responsibility of guarding each person during their life on this earth. They protect the person in the front and from behind from anything that Allah has not decreed. The records of each human being are preserved by the recording angels, who are assigned to a person throughout their lifetime. They write the record of deeds that will be presented on the Day of Judgement. The Angel of Death and his helpers are entrusted with the task of taking the soul of each human at the time of death. There are also angels in charge of the soul during the 'trial in the grave'. They are known by the names *Munkar* and *Nakeer*. They will question the soul in the grave and the final outcome in the hereafter will be made known. There are many other duties that angels are given by Allah.

Belief in angels is an essential element in the belief system of a Muslim. To believe in them means to accept everything that has been related about them in the Qur'an and the Hadith. From these sources, we know some of their attributes, characteristics, names, and responsibilities. We understand their relationship to humankind and their completion of the commands of their Lord. The real significance comes when one comprehends the effect that belief in angels has on the believer. This belief helps one to be patient, dedicated, and obedient to Allah. To know that angels are watching and recording at all times leads the believer to be attentive to every action, wanting to please Allah with his or her deeds. The true believer knows that s/he is not alone on the path to Allah, thus the angels provide security and comfort. There is especially comfort in realizing that no harm can befall the believer except by the will and decree of Allah. Allah has made everything in the universe flow in beautiful synchrony. The angels are part of this and they are intricately entwined in the lives of humankind. They have great benefit for the believer, in bringing comfort to the heart and soul, in guiding to good deeds, and in providing strength to be pious and steadfast.

Connecting Children to the Angels

Children can be connected to angels beginning at a young age as well. In relation to the prophets and revelation, it is necessary for children to believe in angels as they are the link between Allah and His messengers. It would be difficult to believe in the coming of the revelation, particularly the Qur'an, without knowing about and believing in angels. Angel Gabriel, of course, is the angel of revelation and he came to all of the prophets. He came to Prophet Muhammad (bpuh) over a period of twenty-three years. Belief in the angels then (and in Angel Gabriel specifically) is a prerequisite for belief in and confirmation of the Qur'an.

Children can be read stories in which angels spoke to the prophets or other human beings. The most popular story, of course, is when Angel Gabriel came to Prophet Muhammad (bpuh) in the cave of Ḥirâ'. The story of the *isrâ'* and the *mi'râj* (the night journey of the Prophet [bpuh] from Makkah to Jerusalem and then up to visit heaven) would be another example in which Angel Gabriel accompanied the Prophet (bpuh) to the highest heavens. As related in the Qur'an, angels came to various prophets to bring news, such as Prophets Abraham, Zachariah and Lot. There are many other examples.

It is particularly appealing to children to hear the descriptions of angels that reflect Allah's power and ability. In one hadith, for example, it is stated that Angel Gabriel was seen by the Prophet (bpuh) covering the horizon with six hundred wings. Angels can also appear in different forms, such as that of a human being. Children can then begin to relate to the greatness and awe-inspiring nature of Allah's creation. They must believe in these attributes of angels without distorting or trying to depict them in any way.

There are other stories of angels that include valuable lessons. These stories can be used to teach about angels, while at the same time providing children with important morals and values. The following are some examples:

The Prophet (bpuh) said:

«A person visited his brother in another town; Allah deputed an angel to wait for him on his way, and when the man came to him he asked: Where do you intend to go?

He replied: I intend to go to my brother in this town.

The angel asked: Have you done any favour for him (the repayment of which you intend to get)?

He said: No, except for this: that I love him for the sake of Allah, the Exalted and Glorious.

Thereupon he said: I am a messenger to you from Allah (to inform you) that Allah loves you as you love him (for His sake).» (Muslim)

The Prophet (bpuh) said:

«Amongst the Children of Israel there was a man who had murdered ninety-nine persons. He set out asking (whether his repentance could be accepted or not). He came across a monk and asked him if his repentance could be accepted. The monk replied in the negative and so the man killed him. He kept on asking till a man advised him to go to such and such village. (So he left for it) but death overtook him on the way. As he lay dying, he turned his chest towards that village (where he had hoped his repentance would be accepted), and so the angels of mercy and the angels of punishment quarrelled amongst themselves regarding him. Allah ordered the village (towards which he was going) to come closer to him, and ordered the village (whence he had come), to go far away, and then He ordered the angels to measure the distances between his body and the two villages. So he was found to be one span closer to the village (he was going to). So he was forgiven.» (Bukhari)

Abu Hurayrah narrated that he heard the Messenger (bpuh) say:

«Allah willed to test three Israelites who were a leper, a blind man and a bald-headed man. He sent them an angel who came to the leper and said: What would you like most?

The leper replied: Good colour and good skin, for people have a strong aversion to me.

The angel touched him and his illness was cured, and he was given a good colour and beautiful skin.

The angel asked him: What kind of property would you like best?

He replied: Camels (or cows).

(The narrator is in doubt, for either the leper or the bald-headed man demanded camels and the other demanded cows.)

He (the leper) was given a pregnant she-camel, and the angel said (to him): May Allah bless you through it.

The angel then went to the bald-headed man and asked: What would you like most?

He replied: I would like good hair, and wish to be cured of this disease, for people feel repulsion for me.

The angel touched him and his illness was cured, and he was given good hair. The angel asked (him): What kind of property would you like best?

He replied: Cows.

The angel gave him a pregnant cow and said: May Allah bless you through it.

The angel then went to the blind man and asked: What would you like best?

He replied: (I would like) that Allah may restore my eyesight to me so that I may see people.

The angel touched his eyes and Allah gave him back his eyesight. The angel then asked him: What kind of property would you like best?

He replied: Sheep.

The angel gave him a pregnant sheep.

Afterwards, all three pregnant animals gave birth to young ones, and multiplied and brought forth so much that one of the (three) men had a herd of camels filling a valley, and one had a herd of cows filling a valley, and one had a flock of sheep filling a valley.

Then the angel, disguised in the shape and appearance of a leper, went to the leper and said: I am a poor man, who has lost all means of livelihood while on a journey, so none will satisfy my need except Allah and then you. In the name of Him Who has given you such nice colour and beautiful skin, and so much property, I ask you to give me a camel so that I may reach my destination.

The man replied: I have many obligations (so I cannot give you one).

The angel said: I think I know you; were you not a leper to whom people had a strong aversion? Were you not a poor man, and then Allah gave you (all this property)?

The man replied: (This is not so,) I got this property through inheritance from my fore-fathers.

The angel said: If you are telling a lie, then let Allah make you as you were before. Then the angel, disguised in the shape and appearance of a bald man, went to the bald man and said to him the same as he told the first one, and he too answered the same as the first one did.

The angel said: If you are telling a lie, then let Allah make you as you were before.

The angel, disguised as a blind man, went to the blind man and said: I am a poor man and a traveller, whose means of livelihood has been exhausted while on a journey. I have nobody to help me except Allah, and after Him, you yourself. I ask you in the name of Him Who has given you back your eyesight to give me a sheep, so that with its help, I may complete my journey.

The man said: No doubt, I was blind and Allah gave me back my eye-sight; I was poor and Allah made me rich; so take anything you wish from my property. By Allah, I will not stop you from taking anything (you need) of my property, which you may take for Allah's sake.

The angel replied: Keep your property. You all (three men) have been tested, and Allah is pleased with you and is angry with your two companions.» (Bukhari)

These stories from the Hadith help children to strengthen the belief that angels are real and that Allah has a purpose for sending them. They are Allah's emissaries in this life and His sending them means that He cares for His creation and intervenes in their lives as He wishes and during appropriate times. They are a direct connection between Allah and His servants in this world.

The angels, in fact, are responsible for managing the affairs of creation and watching over it. This aspect governs both animate and inanimate objects, laws and principles, as well as *jinn*[30] and humankind. Certain angels are entrusted with the sun and the moon, and yet others with the planets, the clouds, the rain, and the mountains. All of this involves the execution of Allah's preordained decree for all of creation.

Allah has referred to the angels in the following verse:

{Then arrange to do [the Commands of their Lord].}[31]

(Qur'an 79: 5)

Each of the angels is entrusted with different tasks in fulfilment of these commands.

Children readily connect to these concepts, which can be introduced into conversations. When it rains, they may be asked where the rain comes from. They are likely to respond, "Allah." Then they may be asked, "Who follows Allah's command to bring the rain?" They will then respond, "The angels." They can also be told the name of the particular angel, Michael (*Meekâ'eel* in Arabic), who is in charge of this task. These sorts of small reminders work together to confirm and reaffirm belief in Allah and His angels. Even though children are unable to see the angels, they must understand that they are present.

Children should be taught that angels are involved in many aspects of their own lives. This began at the time when they were placed in their mother's womb. Angels were assigned the task of taking care of them while in the uterus of their mother. They, in fact, breathed life into the foetus at the appropriate time and recorded important aspects of the person's life. The Messenger of Allah (bpuh) said:

«The way that each of you is created is that you are gathered in your mother's womb for forty days as a sperm drop, for another forty days as a clot clinging to the inner wall of the womb, and then for a similar length of time as a lump of flesh. Then an angel is sent and he breathes the spirit into you and is charged with four commands: to write down your provision, your lifespan, your actions, and whether you will be wretched or happy.» (Bukhari and Muslim)

When children reach the age of responsibility, angels will begin to record their good and bad deeds and will watch them at all times. The records of each human being are preserved by the recording angels, who are assigned to a person throughout their lifetime. They write the record of deeds that will be presented on the Day of Judgement. Allah has mentioned:

{Or do they think that We hear not their secrets and their private conversations? Yes, [We do], and Our messengers [angels] are with them recording.}

(Qur'an 43: 80)

{And indeed, [appointed] over you are keepers, noble and recording; they know whatever you do.}

(Qur'an 82: 10-12)

Parents should teach young people that each person has two recording angels, one on the left and one on the right. The angel on the left records evil actions and intentions, and the angel on the right records good deeds and intentions. This is evident in the Qur'an:

{When the two receivers [recording angels] receive, seated on the right and on the left. He [a person] does not utter any word except that with him is an observer prepared [to record].}

(Qur'an 50: 17-18)

It is important that young people recognize that angels are also aware of the intentions and the state of the heart of the human. The Messenger of Allah (bpuh) said:

«Allah, the Mighty and Majestic, has said: When My slave wants to do an evil action, you should not write it down until he does it. If he does it, then write down the equivalent of it. If he does not do it for My sake, then write it down as a good action for him. If he wants to do a good action and does not do it, then write it down as a good action. If he does do it, then write down ten to seven hundred of its like.» (Bukhari)

This hadith makes it clear that Allah has given the angels the ability to see and understand the intentions behind the actions of human beings. For young people, this should make them aware that it is not only their deeds that are taken into account, but also their thoughts and intentions.

There are guardian angels that protect humans from whatever has not been decreed for them. They are stationed in front and behind each person.

{For him [each one] are successive [angels] before and behind him who protect him by the decree of Allah.} (Qur'an 13: 11)

Allah has also indicated: {And He is the subjugator over His servants, and He sends over you guardian-angels...}

(Qur'an 6: 61)

These guardian angels have been given the task of protecting the individual until the decree of Allah arrives; then they withdraw from him in order to allow the decree to reach him. They are present until the time of death.[32]

Allah has also appointed an angel as a companion from for each person. The Prophet (bpuh) said:

«There is no one among you but there has been appointed for him one companion from among the jinn and another from among the angels...» (Muslim)

This companion encourages the human to worship Allah, to follow the path of truth and righteousness, and to avoid evil and corruption. The Prophet (bpuh) said:

«The devil has a hold over the son of Adam, and the angel has a hold over him. The hold of the devil tempts a person to do evil and deny the truth. The hold of the angel encourages a person to do good and believe in the truth...»[33] (A 'reliable but odd' hadith recorded by at-Tirmidhi, an-Nasâ'i, and Ibn Ḥibbân; al-Albâni graded it as sound)

Angels supplicate to Allah to send blessings and forgiveness upon the believers. Allah has mentioned:

{It is He who confers blessings upon you, and His angels [ask Him to do so] that He may bring you out from darkness into the light; and ever is He, to the believers, merciful.}

(Qur'an 33:43)

When the angels pray for the believers, this assists them in avoiding disbelief and sin and guides them to the light which is the path of Islam.[34] Children should feel comforted knowing that Allah in His mercy has provided such assistance. Children should be taught that angels will accompany them at the time of their death. The Angel of Death and his helpers are entrusted with the task of taking the soul of each human at the time of death. Allah mentions:

{Say: The angel of death, who has been entrusted with you, will take you. Then to your Lord you will be returned.}

(Qur'an 32: 11)

For the hypocrites and disbelievers, the process will be difficult and repulsive.

{Then how [will it be] when the angels take them in death, striking their faces and their backs?}

(Qur'an 47: 27)

For the believers, it will be pleasant.

{The ones whom the angels take in death, [being] good and pure; [the angels] will say: Peace be upon you. Enter paradise for what you used to do.}

(Qur'an 16: 32)

The appearance of the angels at death is also determined by the condition of the soul at that time. If the person is evil, the angels take on an ugly appearance, a disgusting odour, and a harsh demeanour. For the doer of good, they have the best appearance, the most beautiful form and smell, and will bring the good news in a pleasant manner.

The angels Munkar and Nakeer are in charge of the soul during the trial in the grave. They will question the soul in the grave and the final outcome in the hereafter will be made known. The Prophet (bpuh) said:

«When someone is placed in his grave, and his companions turn and go, and he can still hear the tread of their sandals, two angels come to him and make him sit up and say to him: What do you say about this man, Muhammad, may Allah bless him and grant him peace?

He will say: I testify that he is the slave of Allah and His Messenger.

It will be said: Look at your place in the fire. Allah has given you, in exchange for it, a place in the garden.

The unbeliever or hypocrite will say: I do not know. I used to say what everyone else said.

He will be told: You neither understood nor followed the guidance. Then he will be hit between the ears with an iron hammer and will cry out with a cry which is heard by everything near him except people and jinn.» (Bukhari)

On the Day of Resurrection, the Angel *Isrâfeel* will blow the trumpet to resurrect all the dead from their graves.

Children should be reminded to say "*As-salâmu alaykum*" (peace be with you) when they enter the home, since angels are present and should be greeted. They should understand that reading the Qur'an and studying Islam within the home are very important since they bring the blessings of the angels to the occupants of the home. Attending the mosque for the same purpose is especially beneficial. The Prophet (bpuh) said:

«Whenever people gather in one of the houses of Allah, reciting the Book of Allah and studying it together, tranquillity descends upon them, mercy encompasses them, the angels surround them, and Allah mentions them to those who are with Him.» (Muslim and Abu Dâwood)

Angels of mercy also send blessings on those who visit a sick person.

Ramadan is a particularly opportune time to have discussions about angels. On the Night of Decree,[35] the angels come down from the heavens with the decrees of Allah, as Allah describes,

{The Night of Decree is better than a thousand months. The angels and the Spirit [Gabriel] descend therein by permission of their Lord for every matter.}

(Qur'an 97: 3-4)

This means that they bring down the decree for everything destined to occur in the following year; another important task of the angels of which we should make our children aware.

It is important for children to learn that angels do not enter a house in which there is a statue, or a picture (image of an animate being). The Prophet (bpuh) said:

«The angels do not enter a house in which there is an image.» (Muslim)

This will help them to understand the reason that pictures and figurines of people and animals are not supposed to be displayed in Muslim homes, and assist them in explaining this issue to others who may lack the understanding.

Relating stories and reminding children of their various roles will make angels 'real' or true for them and solidify their faith in this unseen aspect. Young children, in particular, may not completely comprehend something that is invisible, but they begin to imagine in their minds. At this age they also trust what their parents tell them, so there is usually little uncertainty. There may be questions and curiosity, but acceptance comes naturally. We must be certain to convey to them that we may not be able to see angels, but we believe in them because of the many verses of Qur'an and the hadiths of the Prophet (bpuh). Part of faith is to believe in things even though we cannot see them with our own eyes, and revelation has been preserved to prove their existence beyond a shadow of a doubt.

For true connection to the angels and fulfilment of this aspect of eemân, children must develop a deep love for them, knowing that angels are obedient and submissive servants of Allah. As we have a special affection for the believers in this world due to their closeness to Allah, we must also love the angels for the same reason. The angels themselves have a fondness and loyalty to the genuine believers: they pray to Allah for them, ask for their forgiveness, and support them in this life and the hereafter.

Children must come to appreciate that the angels are part of Allah's plan and organization in the universe and they are intricately interwoven into their lives. There is great benefit from this belief in that it brings comfort to the heart and soul, guides to superior actions, and provides the strength to be devout and faithful. It helps one to recognize the majesty of Allah as reflected in the creation of the angels.

It increases one's gratefulness to Allah, to know that He fashioned these creatures to support, protect, and benefit the believers. They bring light, peace, and tranquillity and remove worry, grief, and despair. Angels are truly another of the wonderful and amazing blessings of Allah.

Chapter Eight:
The Prophets and Messengers

{And We send not the messengers except as bringers of good tidings and warners...}

(Qur'an 18: 56)

Belief in the Prophets and Messengers

Belief in prophets and messengers is another of the fundamental principles of Muslims and a component of eemân. Regarding the prophets, Allah mentions,

{Say: We have believed in Allah and in what was revealed to us and what was revealed to Abraham, Ishmael, Isaac, Jacob, and the Descendants,[36] and in what was given to Moses and Jesus, and to the prophets from their Lord. We make no distinction between any of them, and we are Muslims [submitting] to Him.}

(Qur'an 3: 84)

Allah sent a warner to each nation throughout human history, which means that the number of prophets that have come to carry out Allah's mission must be in the hundreds, if not more.

{...And there was no nation but that there had passed within it a warner.}

(Qur'an 35: 24)

Twenty-five prophets and messengers are mentioned by name in the Qur'an: Adam, Idrees (Enoch), Nooḥ (Noah), Hood, Ṣâliḥ, Looṭ (Lot), Ibrâheem (Abraham), Ismâ'eel (Ishmael), Is-ḥâq (Isaac), Ya'qoob (Jacob), Yoosuf (Joseph), Shu'ayb, Hâroon (Aaron), Moosâ (Moses), Dâwood (David), Sulaymân (Solomon), Ayyoob (Job), Dhul-Kifl (Ezekiel), Yoonus (Jonah), Ilyâs (Elias), al-Yas'a (Elisha), Zakariyâ (Zachariah), Yaḥyâ (John), 'Eesâ (Jesus), and Muhammad (bpuh), peace be upon them all.

If a person does not believe in Allah's prophets and messengers, he or she becomes a disbeliever. Allah has specified:

{Indeed, those who disbelieve in Allah and His messengers and wish to discriminate between Allah and His messengers and say: We believe in some and disbelieve in others – wishing to adopt a way in between. Those are the disbelievers, truly...} (Qur'an 4: 150-151)

To disbelieve in even one prophet is equated with disbelieving in all of them. This is due to the fact that to deny the prophets and messengers is to reject their teachings, which is equated with denial of the source of the teachings, the Creator. This leads to failure to achieve the true servitude to Allah that has been enjoined upon humans.

As human beings, we need the messengers and their teachings in order to reform our hearts, enlighten our souls, and guide our minds. We need the messengers in order to give direction to our lives, to connect us to life and to the Creator of life. The scholar Ibn al-Qayyim, explaining the need that people have for the messengers and their teachings, wrote:

> Hence we know that above all else, people need to know about the Messenger and the message he brought, to believe what he told us and to obey what he enjoined upon us, because there is no way to attain happiness and success, either in this world or in the hereafter, except at the hands of the messengers. There is no way to know about good and evil in detail except through them. No one can attain the pleasure of Allah at all except through following their teachings. Good words, deeds and attitudes can only be attained through their guidance and the teachings they brought. They are the standard example: attitudes, manners and actions are to be measured against their words and attitudes. Following them makes the people of misguidance stand out. So our need for them is greater than the body's need for the soul, or the need of the eye for light, or the soul's need for its life. Whatever need or necessity you may think of, a person's need for the messengers is many times greater…Because a person's happiness in this world and in the hereafter is connected to the guidance of the Prophet (bpuh), then each person who is sincere with himself and who wants to attain salvation and happiness has to know enough about his (the Prophet's) teachings, biography and way to ensure that he is not one of those who are ignorant of him so that he be included among his followers and his party.[37]

One aspect of belief in the prophets is to accept that they all called to one religion – the religion of Islam. Allah has mentioned:

{Indeed, the religion according to Allah is Islam.}

(Qur'an 3: 19)

There are several verses that illustrate the fact that all prophets were Muslim. Noah (*'Alayhi as-salâm* – Peace be upon him) said:

{My reward is only from Allah, and I have been commanded to be of the Muslims [those who submit to Allah].}

(Qur'an 10: 72)

With reference to Abraham (bpuh), Allah has informed us:

{When his Lord said to him: Submit, he said: I have submitted [in Islam] to the Lord of the worlds.}

(Qur'an 2: 131)

{And Moses said: O my people, if you have believed in Allah, then rely upon Him, if you should be Muslims [submitting to Him].}

(Qur'an 10: 84)

{The disciples [of Jesus] said: We are supporters for Allah. We have believed in Allah and testify that we are Muslims [submitting to Him].}

(Qur'an 3: 52)

In essence, 'Islam' or 'submission' was a common word spoken by Allah's prophets from ancient times until now.

The final prophet and messenger is Muhammad (bpuh). He is the Seal of the Prophets, as there will be no other prophet after him.

{...but [he is] the Messenger of Allah and the seal [last] of the prophets.}

(Qur'an 33: 40)

While other prophets were sent to specific nations or groups and for particular eras in human history, Prophet Muhammad (bpuh) was the only prophet sent to all of humankind until the end of time. The sacred Book, the Qur'an, given to Prophet Muhammad (bpuh) will be preserved until the Day of Judgement.

For this reason Prophet Muhammad (bpuh) has a special status. He said:

«I will be the leader of the children of Adam on the Day of Resurrection, and I am not boasting. In my hand there will be a banner of praise, and I am not boasting. There will be no prophet that day, Adam or anyone else, but he will be beneath my banner. I will be the first one to intercede and the first one to be called upon to intercede, and I am not boasting.» (A sound hadith narrated by Aḥmad, at-Tirmidhi and Ibn Mâjah)

He was given special favours and blessings from Allah. The Prophet (bpuh) said:

«I have been favoured over the prophets with six things: I have been given concise speech; I have been supported with fear (of me, cast in the hearts of my enemies); the spoils of war have been made permissible to me; the earth has been made a means of purification and a place of worship for me; I have been sent to all humanity; and I am the last of the prophets.» (Muslim and at-Tirmidhi)

Connecting Children to the Prophets and Messengers

As children are connected to angels through storytelling, the same can be utilized in respect to the prophets. There are many authenticated stories from Qur'an and the Hadith regarding the prophets, as well as an abundance of children's books on these stories. Learning can also be made fun by the use of games, computer programs, and so forth. Children should regularly be exposed to this information and be taught to love the prophets, and in particular, Prophet Muhammad (bpuh). Children should understand that prophets are a mercy to humankind, for they bring the message of Allah and Islam to the people. They are special individuals who were chosen by Allah for this noble mission. They provide the most excellent example of how to live in this life and are the ideal role models for our children.

Children will listen with excitement and curiosity to the story of Noah (bpuh) and the great flood, the story of Abraham (bpuh) and how he was thrown into the fire for breaking the idols, the story of Moses (bpuh) and how he was saved from Pharaoh and his soldiers, the story of Jonah (bpuh) in the stomach of the whale, the story of Joseph (bpuh) and his eventual reunion with his family, the story of Jesus (bpuh) and his miraculous birth, and so many other narratives that are all the more fascinating because the Qur'an has documented them and attested to their truth.

Special love and affection should be given to Prophet Muhammad (bpuh) by the believers. Loving the Prophet (bpuh) is one of the obligatory duties in Islam. Children should be taught to love the Prophet (bpuh) more than their own selves and everything else in this world. Their love for him should be second only to love for Allah. Allah informs us,

{The Prophet is more worthy of the believers than themselves...}

(Qur'an 33: 6)

The Prophet (bpuh) said:

«None of you believes until he loves me more than he loves his own father, his own child, and all other people.» (Bukhari and Muslim)

'Abdullâh ibn Hishâm said:

«We were with the Prophet (bpuh) and he was holding the hand of 'Umar ibn al-Khaṭṭâb. 'Umar said: O Messenger of Allah, you are dearer to me than everything except my own self.

The Messenger (bpuh) said: No, by Him in Whose Hands is my soul, (you will not have complete faith) till I am dearer to you than your own self.

'Umar said: Then, by Allah you are dearer to me than my own self.

The Prophet (bpuh) said: Now, 'Umar (now you are a believer).» (Bukhari)

A child must understand that the strength of love for the Messenger (bpuh) is connected to his or her level of eemân. When his or her faith increases, his or her love for the Prophet (bpuh) increases, and vice versa. Love for the Prophet Muhammad (bpuh) is thus a measure of one's faith and inner conviction. This love for the Prophet (bpuh) is an act of obedience to Allah and a means of drawing closer to Him.

As part of this love and respect, children should become familiar with the etiquette of sending blessings upon the Prophet (bpuh) whenever his name is mentioned. This is an order from Allah. He has declared:

{Indeed, Allah confers blessing upon the Prophet, and His angels [ask Him to do so]. O you who have believed, ask [Allah to confer] blessing upon him and ask [Allah to grant him] peace.}

(Qur'an 33: 56)

In this verse, Allah and His angels are honouring the Prophet (bpuh), and Allah requests the believers to do the same. For this reason, we continually send prayers and blessings upon him.

Another aspect of loving the Prophet (bpuh) is to follow his example. Allah has indicated:

{Say [O Muhammad]: If you should love Allah, then follow me, [so] Allah will love you and forgive you your sins. And Allah is Forgiving and Merciful.}

(Qur'an 3: 31)

To follow means to love, to honour, to obey, and to emulate. The best model for people in all matters is Prophet Muhammad (bpuh). It is our duty as parents to instruct our children in his teachings and the importance of obeying him. Allah has declared:

{O you who have believed, obey Allah and obey the Messenger and those in authority among you. And if you disagree over anything, refer it to Allah and the Messenger, if you should believe in Allah and the Last Day. That is the best [way] and best in result.}

(Qur'an 4: 59)

{Say (O Muhammad): If you should love Allah, then follow me, [so] Allah will love you and forgive you your sins. And Allah is Forgiving and Merciful.}

(Qur'an 3: 31)

Several verses in the Qur'an may be used to highlight this important aspect of Islam. Obedience to the Prophet (bpuh) is, in actuality, obedience to Allah.

{He who obeys the Messenger has obeyed Allah…}

(Qur'an 4: 80)

In addition, the Prophet (bpuh) said:

«Whoever obeys me, obeys Allah. Whoever disobeys me, disobeys Allah.» (Bukhari and Muslim)

In practical terms, children should be taught the Sunnah of the Prophet (bpuh) in all areas of life. This can be accomplished through learning the hadiths of the Prophet (bpuh). Children should be encouraged to memorize hadiths along with the Qur'an. This can begin at an early age with short hadiths. The meaning of the hadiths must also be emphasized. The Prophet's Sunnah should be followed in word and deed so that it is the path they follow throughout their entire lives. His example should be implemented in all aspects of life – eating, sleeping, praying, working, and even playing. Appropriate supplications should be memorized for the various occasions. Children should be proudly reminded that they are following the Prophet's example when they engage in these particular behaviours and supplications. The Prophet (bpuh) should be their ideal role model.

When decisions need to be made or problems are encountered, children should be encouraged to research the Qur'an and the Hadith for possible answers or solutions. They are our best guidance for how to deal with various problems and issues in our lives. There must be trust that following these sources is the best thing for this life.

If the answers are not there, there may at least be some indication as to the direction that should be taken. As with the Sunnah, the prayer for guidance should be made when important decisions are made.

In order to instil love of the Prophet (bpuh) in children, it will be indispensable for them to learn about his seerah, or life story. Regular sessions or family times should be established for this purpose, or it can be integrated into a weekly home study circle. There are many books available for children in the Arabic and English languages, as well as in other languages. Appropriate material should be selected based upon the ages and developmental levels of the children.

Through the seerah, they will discover the character and traits of this great man, the message that he conveyed, and the ways in which he sacrificed for the sake of the community. They will learn of his bravery and courage as he strived to defend and propagate Islam. They will hear about the numerous miracles bestowed by Allah upon him as an indication of his role as prophet of Islam. They will discover how the Companions of the Prophet (bpuh), even young Companions, responded to his call, obeyed his commands, and fought those who attempted to harm him and the message. This knowledge will increase their fondness, attachment, and belief in him. It will bring them closer to him and increase their desire to follow his example in life. It will enhance their connection to the Qur'an and the meanings of the Qur'an, as the Hadith and the Sunnah provide more detailed explanation of our holy Book. In essence, it will stir up their emotions and have a wondrous effect upon their souls and their eemân.

Chapter Nine:
The Books and Revelation

The Prophet (bpuh) said:

«The best discourse is the Book of Allah and the best example is the example of Muhammad.» (Muslim)

Belief in the Books and Revelation

The fourth basic principle of faith is to believe with conviction in the messages that Allah revealed through His prophets and messengers. Allah has informed us:

{Say [O believers]: We have believed in Allah and what has been revealed to us and what has been revealed to Abraham and Ishmael and Isaac and Jacob and the Descendants, and what was given to Moses and Jesus and what was given to the prophets from their Lord. We make no distinction between any of them, and we are Muslims [in submission] to Him.}

(Qur'an 2: 136)

{...say: I have believed in what Allah has revealed of scripture [the Qur'an], and I have been commanded to do justice among you...}

(Qur'an 42: 15)

The messages brought to people by the prophets and messengers were all revealed from Allah. The essence of the calls of all messengers and messages was to tawḥeed – to the worship of Allah alone with no partner or associate. This is clearly detailed in the Qur'an. Allah has indicated:

{And We did not send before you any messenger] except that We revealed to him: There is none worthy of worship except Me, so worship Me.}

(Qur'an 21: 25)

The stories of the prophets illustrate this point further: Prophet Noah (pbuh):

{...O my people, worship Allah; you have no deity other than Him...}

(Qur'an 7: 59)

Prophet Abraham (pbuh):

{...Worship Allah, and fear Him. That is best for you if you should know.}

(Qur'an 29: 16)

Prophet Hood (pbuh):

{...O my people, worship Allah; you have no deity other than Him...}

(Qur'an 7: 65)

Prophet Ṣâliḥ (pbuh):

{...O my people, worship Allah; you have no deity other than Him...}

(Qur'an 7: 73)

Revelation also demonstrates to humans the true path and way of life that is pleasing to Allah. When one knows Allah, there is a desire to know how to please Him and avoid His displeasure. This is mentioned each day in the prayer:

{Guide us to the straight path—the path of those upon whom You have bestowed favour, not of those who have evoked [Your] anger or of those who are astray.}

(Qur'an 1: 6-7)

This leads to proper behaviour, manners, and character, and develops a complete and balanced Islamic personality.

As a component of belief, a believer accepts as true what was said in previously revealed messages, and that ruling according to them was obligatory upon the nations to whom the books were sent. However, s/he does not believe in the existing books held sacred by the Jews and Christians, due to numerous changes and distortions that have been introduced by people over the centuries. In addition, previous messages were connected to particular times and groups, and thus their rulings were only temporary. Allah did not guarantee to preserve them; rather He entrusted this task to the rabbis and priests of each nation. They were unable to preserve their books and betrayed their trust by altering and distorting their content.

The sacred book of Muslims, the Qur'an, is the final message that encompasses or abrogates that which was written in the Torah and the Gospels. The Qur'an is a general message for all of humankind since Muhammad (bpuh) is the Seal of the Prophets. It is distinct from other messages in that it is suitable for all times and places, as it transcends circumstances and eras.

It is addressed to human nature, which does not alter or change, by providing holistic and general rulings as well as detailed laws. Every aspect of life is dealt with in one way or another.

{…And We have sent down to you the Book as clarification for all things and as guidance and mercy and good tidings for the Muslims.}

(Qur'an 16: 89)

A mu'min not only believes in the Qur'an as a comprehensive guide, but also follows its commandments and heeds its prohibitions.

Unlike previous scriptures, Allah has guaranteed to preserve the Qur'an. He did not entrust this task to human beings, but rather promised that He Himself would protect it. Allah says,

{Indeed, it is We who sent down the message [the Qur'an], and indeed, We will be its guardian.}

(Qur'an 15: 9)

A testimony to the truth of this is that the Qur'an has been preserved in both written and oral form. The written book has never been altered, and millions of people around the world have memorized the Qur'an by heart.

The purpose and goals of revelation include teaching the creation about Allah, His oneness and His attributes. It answers the basic questions of humans such as "Who is my Creator and God?", "What is my relationship to Him?", and "Why did He create me?" This knowledge can never be learned from any other source. The more one knows about Allah, the more one will have love, hope and fear in Allah.

Connecting Children to Revelation

Children should learn to love the Qur'an, Allah's speech and revelation to humankind. This love is connected to one's love for Allah and His Messenger. 'Abdullâh ibn Mas'ood said, "Whoever wishes to love Allah and His Messenger should read the Qur'an." (A reliable hadith narrated by al-Bayhaqi and Abu Nu'aym)

Connection with the Qur'an on a continual basis is one of the main paths to development of love, fear, and hope in Allah; it is one of the keys to nurturing eemân.

Children should have the correct belief that the Qur'an is revealed from Allah and that it is the speech and word of Allah. They should have no doubt that everything stated in the Qur'an is true and perfect. They should be pleased with it and submit to it completely.

They must understand that to ridicule, doubt or reject even one verse of the Qur'an is a very serious matter. In fact, rejection of one verse of the Qur'an entails negation of belief in Allah's revelation.

Respect and reverence for the Qur'an should be taught from a young age, through modelling and direct instruction. Children should learn the appropriate manners for reciting the Qur'an. This includes choosing the proper time for recitation, particularly when one will be free from distractions and interruptions. A proper place and atmosphere for recitation should also be chosen, such as a special place in the home where one is less likely to be disturbed. They should sit in a way that gives respect to the Qur'an, including facing the direction for prayer. It would be appropriate to make ablution and the proper intention before reading. And one should always seek refuge from Satan, as mentioned in the Book:

{So when you recite the Qur'an, [first] seek refuge in Allah from Satan, the expelled [from His mercy.}

(Qur'an 16: 95)

Love of the Qur'an must not be only with the heart and tongue, but also shown in actions toward the Qur'an. Children should recite, study, and memorize the Qur'an on a regular basis. Memorization of the Qur'an may begin as young as two or three years of age with small chapters. This should not be carried out as a chore, but rather as an opportunity to get closer to Allah and to elevate one's status in this life and the hereafter. Appropriate hadiths regarding the eminence bestowed upon those who exert effort toward the Qur'an should be shared with children. This will provide encouragement and enhance their self-esteem. The Messenger of Allah (bpuh) said:

«The best amongst you is the one who learns the Qur'an and teaches it.» (Bukhari)

He also said:

«A person who recites the Qur'an and masters it by heart will be with the noble righteous scribes (in heaven). And if such a person exerts himself to learn the Qur'an by heart, and recites it with great difficulty, will have a double reward.» (Bukhari)

The Prophet (bpuh) also provided an analogy regarding the merit of reciting Qur'an:

«The example of a believer who recites the Qur'an and acts on it is like a citron which tastes nice and smells nice. And the example of a believer who does not recite the Qur'an but acts on it is like a date which tastes good but has no smell. And the example of a hypocrite who recites the Qur'an is like basil, which smells good but tastes bitter. And the example of a hypocrite who does not recite the Qur'an is like a colocynth (bitter melon), which tastes bitter and has a bad smell.» (Bukhari and Abu Dâwood)

Along with recitation and memorization, children should begin to study explanations of the Qur'an to comprehend the meaning of the verses. Recitation has limited benefit without the understanding that must accompany it. It is for this reason that it should be read under the most appropriate circumstances for learning. The purpose of reading the Qur'an is to ponder over it and to absorb the wisdom and guidance that it contains, as Allah has mentioned:

{Then do they not reflect upon the Qur'an, or are there locks upon [their] hearts?}

(Qur'an 47: 24)

Some scholars even say that reading less of the Qur'an with concentration and understanding is better than reading more while not comprehending. The goal should be to understand, believe completely, and then apply it in one's life.

It must be made clear that the Qur'an should be given full attention while reading, as this was the method of the Prophet (bpuh). When the reader comes across a verse regarding a matter or an order that they have not fulfilled properly, they should ask Allah for forgiveness and assistance to improve in this aspect. When s/he reads a verse concerning Allah's mercy, s/he should respond by asking Allah for such mercy. When Allah's punishment is mentioned, s/he should seek refuge in Allah from that. Reading in this manner will increase faith in one's heart.

{The believers are only those who, when Allah is mentioned, their hearts become fearful, and when His verses are recited to them, it increases them in faith; and they rely upon their Lord.}

(Qur'an 8: 2)

Learning the Arabic language, of course, is an absolute necessity and an obligation upon parents to teach their children. A person can never truly connect with the Qur'an without knowing and understanding its language of transmission. Translations of the meanings of the Qur'an are useful, but fall short in conveying the beauty, intensity, and magnificence of the Arabic text. Arabic is a unique language that is superior to any other language in the world.

It is an honour for Muslims to be blessed with such an incredible gift. A child who learns this language from birth will carry the gift throughout his or her lifetime.

An appropriate place to start with young children in terms of understanding the Qur'an is the stories and parables that are contained within it. The stories of the prophets are simple and easy for young children to follow and appreciate. They are spread throughout the Qur'an in various forms and styles, and thus are easily accessible. The complete chapter of Joseph (*Soorat*[38] *Yoosuf*), for example, is a story in itself, relating events that occurred in the life of Prophet Joseph (bpuh). It is a beautiful, poignant account that contains many valuable messages. There are also other stories contained in the Qur'an, such as that of the two men and their gardens in the chapter of the cave (*Soorat al-Kahf*).

It is important that children realize that these stories are not fables, but rather true events that occurred in the history of civilization. As Muslims, we accept and believe these facts since they are preserved in Allah's noble Book. The stories and parables in the Qur'an contain lessons for humankind with which children can also begin to become familiar. As they get older, the more profound meanings will become apparent to them, but at least the groundwork will have been laid at a young age.

Children and youth must also be taught to act in accordance with the rulings and guidance of the Qur'an. There is really no benefit if a person does not seek to obey and implement the guidance of the Qur'an in life. It was narrated that Abu 'Abdur-Raḥmân (*Raḍiya Allâhu 'Anhu* - May Allah be pleased with him) said: "The Companions of the Prophet (bpuh) who used to teach us the Qur'an told us that they would learn ten verses, then they would not move on to the next ten verses until they had learned the knowledge contained therein and how to act upon it. They said, "So we learned that knowledge and how to put it into practice." (Recorded by al-Ḥâkim with a sound chain)

This is corroborated by an authentic hadith in which Abdullâh ibn Mas'ood said, "When one among us learned ten verses, he would not go beyond them until he knew their meanings and he acted upon them." Parents, of course, provide the best model in this regard.

It must be understood that one's honour and distinction are only found in adhering to and applying the Qur'an. Islam is the path to true happiness in life and the Qur'an is the light that guides the person along the way.

The Prophet (bpuh) said:

«O people, certainly I am but a human and soon a messenger from my Lord may come to me and I will respond to his call [and die]. I am leaving among you two heavy things. The first of them is the Book of Allah. It contains guidance and light. The one who misses adhering to it shall go astray. Therefore, take the Book of Allah and cling to it...» (Aḥmad and Muslim)

Teaching your child the Qur'an means that you are giving them the greatest blessing of a lifetime. It will set them apart from other people and make them special in the eyes of Allah.

{Indeed, We have sent down for you a Book in which there is your honour and distinction (for the one who follows it). Will you not then understand?}

(Qur'an 21: 10)

«The Prophet (bpuh) said: Certainly, Allah has special people among humankind.

They asked: O Messenger of Allah, who are they?

He replied: They are the people of the Qur'an – they are the people of Allah and specially His.» (A sound hadith narrated by Aḥmad, Ibn Mâjah, and an-Nasâ'i)

The Qur'an will bring peace, tranquillity and Allah's mercy to their lives. The Prophet (bpuh) said:

«Whoever follows a path in order to seek knowledge thereby, Allah will make easy for him, due to it, a path to paradise. No people gather in a house of Allah, reciting the Book of Allah and studying it among themselves, except that tranquillity descends upon them, mercy covers them, the angels surround them, and Allah makes mention of them to those in His presence...» (Muslim)

As Allah mentions in *Soorat ar-Raḥmân*, He bestowed the Qur'an upon humans as a mercy from Himself:

{The Most Merciful, taught the Qur'an, created the human.}

(Qur'an 55: 1-3)

So too, it is a mercy for parents (from Allah's mercy) to impart this wisdom to their children. In fact, it is the greatest mercy that can be bestowed upon them. The Qur'an will be their guide and protection throughout life, and its constant reminders will have a profound effect upon their eemân and commitment to Islam.

{And the horn will be blown; and at once from the graves to their Lord they will hasten. They will say: O woe to us! Who has raised us up from our sleeping place? [The reply will be:] This is what the Most Merciful had promised, and the messengers told the truth.}

(Qur'an 36: 51-52)

Chapter Ten:

The Day of Resurrection and the Hereafter

Belief in the Day of Resurrection and the Hereafter

Belief in the Day of Resurrection and the hereafter is the fifth pillar of eemân. This entails belief in all related concepts, including the trial and questioning in the grave, the torment and bliss of the grave, the resurrection, the gathering, the records, the reckoning, the scale, the fount, the bridge, intercession, paradise and hellfire, and everything that Allah has prepared for those who dwell within them. A Muslim believes in all that is mentioned in the Qur'an and the Hadith regarding these topics, without addition or change.

The Last Day is mentioned in the Qur'an on numerous occasions and in various literary styles. Allah has mentioned:

{Righteousness is not that you turn your faces toward the east or the west, but [true] righteousness is [in] one who believes in Allah, the Last Day, the angels, the Book, and the prophets...}

(Qur'an 2: 177)

{...And whoever disbelieves in Allah, His angels, His books, His messengers, and the Last Day has certainly gone far astray.}

(Qur'an 4: 136)

{Indeed, the Hour is coming – I almost conceal it – so that every soul may be recompensed according to that for which it strives. So do not let one avert you from it who does not believe in it and follows his desire, for you [then] would perish.}

(Qur'an 20: 15-16)

A great deal of detail is provided on this subject, which is unique in comparison to other issues of the unseen. The Last Day is referred to by many names, often describing the events that will occur on that day. Some of the names mentioned in the Qur'an, for example, include: Day of Resurrection, Day of Reckoning, Day of Rising, the Striking Hour, the Overwhelming, and so on.

Belief in the Last Day is without doubt. Allah has mentioned:

{Allah – there is no deity except Him. He will surely assemble you for [account on] the Day of Resurrection, about which there is no doubt. And who is more truthful than Allah in statement?}

(Qur'an 4: 87)

{Those who disbelieve have claimed that they will never be resurrected. Say: Yes, by my Lord, you will surely be resurrected; then you will surely be informed of what you did. And that, for Allah, is easy.}

(Qur'an 64: 7)

To establish its importance even further, belief in the Last Day is often connected to belief in Allah. Allah has specified:

{…but [true] righteousness is [in] one who believes in Allah, the Last Day, the angels, the Book, and the prophets…}

(Qur'an 2: 177)

{…That is instructed to whoever of you believes in Allah and the Last Day…}

(Qur'an 2: 232)

Prophet Shu'ayb (bpuh) said to his people:

{…O my people, worship Allah and expect the Last Day and do not commit abuse on the earth, spreading corruption.}

(Qur'an 29: 36)

There are many such examples in the Qur'an of this connection between belief in Allah and belief in the Last Day.

These reminders of the events of the Day of Resurrection and the life in the hereafter should have an influence on the thoughts and behaviour of the believer. A person who believes that s/he will be judged and brought to account will conduct himself or herself within the constraints of goodness, piety, truth, and justice. This is the reason that, in the Qur'an, righteous deeds are often associated with belief in the Last Day. Allah mentions:

{…Those who believe in the Hereafter believe in it, and they are maintaining their prayers.}

(Qur'an 6: 92)

{There has certainly been for you in them an excellent pattern for anyone whose hope is in Allah and the Last Day. And whoever turns away – then indeed, Allah is the Free of need, the Praiseworthy.}

(Qur'an 60: 6)

{Those who believe in Allah and the Last Day would not ask permission of you to be excused from striving [fighting] with their wealth and their lives. And Allah is Knowing of those who fear Him. Only those would ask permission of you who do not believe in Allah and the Last Day and whose hearts have doubted, and they, in their doubt, are hesitating.}

(Qur'an 9: 44-45)

This sets the believer apart from the person who denies that s/he will be resurrected and judged for his or her actions in this life; one who is preoccupied by worldly desires and ambitions and his or her own personal interests. Allah has mentioned:

{But they wonder that there has come to them a warner from among themselves, and the disbelievers say: This is an amazing thing. When we have died and have become dust, [will we return to life]? That is a distant [unlikely] return.}

(Qur'an 50: 2-3)

{And they say: There is not but our worldly life; we die and live, and nothing destroys us except time. And they have of that no knowledge; they are only assuming.}

(Qur'an 45: 24)

Disbelief in the Day of Resurrection brings misery to the human and leads him or her to deviate from his or her intended path in this life. One who rejects the possibility of resurrection, in effect, disbelieves in all of Allah's Messengers, since all of them had brought an account of these matters. Allah has responded to their disbelief in the resurrection and hereafter in the Qur'an:

{And they say: When we are bones and crumbled particles, will we [truly] be resurrected as a new creation? Say: Be you stones or iron, or [any] creation of that which is great within your breasts. And they will say: Who will restore us? Say: He who brought you forth the first time. Then they will nod their heads toward you and say: When is that? Say: Perhaps it will be soon.}

(Qur'an 17: 49-51)

Connecting Children to the Day of Resurrection and the Hereafter

Children can be connected to belief in the hereafter in a variety of ways. As this topic is mentioned throughout the Qur'an, this would obviously be the proper tool for approaching the subject matter. Children are able to accept and understand the concepts of death, resurrection, and an afterlife, depending on their particular level of development. These are issues that should be discussed freely and comfortably within the home.

In the Qur'an, for example, Allah provides similes of death and resurrection so that the reader may more easily comprehend. This can be particularly effective for children since it ties abstract concepts to something more tangible. By nature children are concrete thinkers, so they are in need of such techniques to assist in their understanding. As they enter adolescence, the ability to appreciate abstract notions becomes apparent.

One of the greatest proofs that Allah uses in the Qur'an for the resurrection after death is that of our own creation. If Allah was able to create us in the first place, it will be even easier to re-create us on the Day of Resurrection. Children should be reminded that their existence and their creation are from Allah and that He will return them to Him. Allah has mentioned:

{And the [disbelieving] human says: When I have died, am I going to be brought forth alive? Does man not remember that We created him before, while he was nothing?}

(Qur'an 19: 66-67)

The initial creation of human beings is a reminder of this. Allah has detailed:

{O people, if you should be in doubt about the resurrection, then [consider that] indeed, We created you from dust, then from a sperm-drop, then from a clinging clot, and then from a lump of flesh, formed and unformed – that We may show you. And We settle in the wombs whom We will for a specified term, then We bring you out as a child, and then [We develop you] that you may reach your [time of] maturity. And among you is he who is taken in [early] death, and among you is he who is returned to the most decrepit [old] age so that he knows, after [once having] knowledge, nothing. And you see the earth barren, but when We send down upon it rain, it quivers and swells and grows [something] of every beautiful kind. That is because Allah is the Truth and because He gives life to the dead and because He is over all things competent. And [that they may know] that the Hour is coming – no doubt about it – and that Allah will resurrect those in the graves.}

(Qur'an 22: 5-7)

In this verse, Allah coins a parable of resurrection of the dead by likening it to how He revives the earth with vegetation after it has been barren. This same parable can be found in several places in the Qur'an. Allah has mentioned:

{And of His signs is that you see the earth stilled, but when We send down upon it rain, it quivers and grows. Indeed, He who has given it life is the Giver of Life to the dead. Indeed, He is competent over all things.}

(Qur'an 41: 39)

{And who sends down rain from the sky in measured amounts, and We revive thereby a dead land – thus will you be brought forth.}

(Qur'an 43: 11)

Children relate easily to features of nature, so these types of parables can be very effective. Parents should encourage them to ponder the wonders of nature and how the land is brought back to life after its death. This is truly an amazing phenomenon that we often take for granted. The seasons of the year are a sign of Allah's power and majesty, and a reminder of our own death and resurrection. We should not allow them to pass without taking notice and being grateful for Allah's bounties. The whole creation itself is reminder of the ability of Allah to create and re-create.

{Have they not considered how Allah begins creation and then repeats it? Indeed that, for Allah, is easy. Say [O Muhammad]: Travel through the land and observe how He began creation. Then Allah will produce the final creation [development]. Indeed, Allah, over all things, is competent.}

(Qur'an 29: 19-20)

{And it is He who begins creation; then He repeats it, and that is [even] easier for Him. To Him belongs the highest description [attribute] in the heavens and earth. And He is the Exalted in Might, the Wise.}

(Qur'an 30: 27)

Allah has created this vast universe; would it not then be within His ability to create something less significant, which is the human being?

{Is not He who created the heavens and the earth Able to create the likes of them? Yes, [it is so]; and He is the Knowing Creator. His command is only when He intends a thing that He says to it: Be!—and it is. So Exalted is He in whose hand is the realm of all things, and to Him you will be returned.} (Qur'an 36: 81-83)

A family's vacation trip can easily be turned into a lesson integrating these verses and signs. A garden in the backyard can be a daily opportunity to remind children of Allah's might and bounties. Studies in science should consistently be tied to verses from the Qur'an and hadiths of the Prophet (bpuh) so that children realize that the miracles of science exist only by the will of Allah. Humans have no power or ability compared to that which Allah possesses. Many scientists in current times disregard this fact due to their failure to connect knowledge and discoveries to the power and might of Allah.

Death

The death of a loved one or family friend would be an appropriate occasion to discuss the issues of death and the afterlife with a child. The discussion should be candid, but should also fit the developmental stage of the child. Regardless of the age, children can be told that everyone, including themselves, will die at some time. Children should understand, however, that their loved one is not gone, but has only passed on to the next phase of existence. Death is only a stage that s/he has passed through, as we all will one day. S/he will be raised again on the Day of Resurrection with his or her family and all other humans. Rather than grieving and being sad for this person, there should be an element of joy that they have gone on to meet their Lord. Older children may be provided information regarding the barrier or interval before the Day of Resurrection, and life in the grave. They may also be taken to graves as a further reminder of the reality.

Death is not a negative thing from the perspective of Islam and it should not be portrayed as such. Children should not develop worry or fear of death. Rather, they should be encouraged to discuss the issue and think about it often. The Prophet (bpuh) actually encouraged the believers to do this. He said:

«Remember often the destroyer of pleasure, death, for no one remembers death in times of hardship but that it makes him feel better, and no one remembers death in times of ease but that it restrains him.» (Recorded by al-Haythami with a reliable chain: authenticated by al-Albâni)

Sleep itself is a form of 'lesser death'. Waking from sleep is a type of resurrection. Children can be reminded of this fact. Allah has mentioned:

{And it is He who takes your souls by night and knows what you have committed by day. Then He revives you therein [by day] that a specified term may be fulfilled. Then to Him will be your return; then He will inform you about what you used to do.}

(Qur'an 6: 60)

{Allah takes the souls at the time of their death, and those that do not die [He takes] during their sleep. Then He keeps those for which He has decreed death and releases the others for a specified term. Indeed in that are signs for a people who give thought.}

(Qur'an 39: 42)

During sleep, Allah takes the souls. If He wishes, He may keep the soul; and if He wills that the person should remain alive, He returns the soul. The supplications made upon rising from sleep and before going to sleep mention this fact. Upon awakening, children should recite the following supplication:

"All praise is for Allah Who gave us life after having taken it from us, and unto Him is the resurrection. (*Alḥamdulillâh alladhee aḥyânâ ba'da mâ amâtanâ wa ilayhin-nushoor.*)" (Bukhari)

The following supplication should be said before going to sleep:

"In Your name my Lord, I lie down and in Your name I rise, so if You should take my soul then have mercy upon it, and if You should return my soul then protect as You protect Your righteous servants. (*Bismika Rabbee waḍa'tu janbee, wa bika arfa'uhu, fa in amsakta nafsee farḥamhâ, wa in arsaltahâ faḥfadh-hâ bi mâ taḥfudhu bihi 'ibâdak aṣ-ṣâliḥeen.*)" (Bukhari and Muslim)

Children should understand the meaning of these supplications and their relationship to death and resurrection.

It is the habit of righteous people to remind themselves and others about death. This assists the believer in remaining constantly prepared for his or her own death, since the exact moment is unknown. To be prepared means to have correct belief, to be consistent and persistent in performance of religious obligations, and to hasten in the performance of righteous deeds. In essence, remembrance of death leads a person to strive to reform and purify himself or herself. This is one of the main purposes of the message of Islam.

Responsibility and Accountability

One of the key aspects of parenting is to teach children that they are responsible for their actions and that one day they will be brought to account before Allah. Allah has mentioned this fact in the Qur'an: {Every soul, for what it has earned, will be held retained [subject or held responsible].} (Qur'an 74: 38)

The individual will stand alone on that day.

{And all of them are coming to Him on the Day of Resurrection alone.}

(Qur'an 19: 95)

There will be no one to speak on his or her behalf or to defend him or her, not even close family members or friends.

{On the day a man will flee from his brother, and his mother and his father, and his wife and his children; for every person, that day, will be a matter adequate [to occupy] him for him. He will be concerned only with himself, thus forgetting all others.}

(Qur'an 80: 34-37)

The only evidence to allow entrance into paradise will be belief in Allah and His Messenger and good deeds.

This understanding will prove invaluable for discipline and behaviour management of a child. Self-control is something that must come from within and this is exactly the outcome of belief in the Day of Resurrection and the hereafter. It must be imprinted on the minds of children that Allah will weigh the deeds of a person and reward those whose deeds are heavy; those whose deeds are light will not be successful. Allah has mentioned:

{And the weighing [of deeds] that Day will be the truth. So those whose scales are heavy – it is they who will be successful. And those whose scales are light – they are the ones who will lose themselves for what injustice they were doing toward Our signs and verses.}

(Qur'an 7: 8-9)

The Nature of this World

In this way, children will realize that the purpose of this life is only as a preparation for the next. They will use it to prepare themselves for the hereafter and the foremost test that awaits them. They will strive to increase the weighing of their scales in order to have the best outcome. This will become their primary goal and that which they continually endeavour to achieve. Other goals in their worldly life become secondary to this central aspiration.

Children should also understand that Allah sometimes tests us in various ways to determine if we are deserving of His rewards in the hereafter.

{[He] who created death and life to test you [as to] which of you is best in deed – and He is the Exalted in Might, the Forgiving.} (Qur'an 67: 2)

{Do the people think that they will be left to say: We believe. –And they will not be tried? But We have certainly tried those before them, and Allah will surely make evident those who are truthful, and He will surely make evident the liars.}

(Qur'an 29: 2-3)

The stories of the Prophet (bpuh) and his Companions may be useful in this regard. They suffered severe physical and mental hardship in order to prove their sincerity to Allah and their commitment to Islam.

When children understand the temporal nature of this world and the fact that it will eventually come to an end, this diminishes their interest in the material things and decreases love of this life. When they realize that this world is temporary and not our permanent abode, it will become less significant to them. This is one of the characteristics of a true believer. In this way, they will not covet, work for, or compete over matters of this worldly life, as do those who create their own 'paradise' in the life of this world and focus on that as an end in itself. They will not waste their time in idle and trivial pursuits, but rather will use their time wisely, for the sake of Allah. They will set their goal for what is awaiting them in the hereafter. They will be able to delay gratification in this world for that which will come in the next, realizing that the recompense in the hereafter is eternal. 'Abdullâh ibn 'Umar said:

«The Messenger of Allah (bpuh) took hold of my shoulder and said: Be in this world as if you were a stranger or a traveller.

The sub-narrator added: Ibn 'Umar used to say: If you survive till the evening, do not expect to be alive in the morning, and if you survive till the morning, do not expect to be alive in the evening, and take from your health for your sickness, and (take) from your life for your death.» (Bukhari)

Obviously someone who travels tends to travel lightly; they only take for the journey what is absolutely necessary. As the Prophet (bpuh) advised, we should exist in this world in the same manner, avoiding the 'piling up' of goods and material things. This is a useful analogy to use with children and it contains important lessons.

Another simile that can be presented to children is mentioned in the following hadith. The Prophet (bpuh) said:

«The world is a prison for a believer and paradise for a disbeliever.» (Muslim)

A prison conjures up images of discomfort, gloominess, and restriction of freedom. It is a place from which a person would wish to escape. As such is the residence on this earth. A believer will desire to leave this place as s/he knows about the treasures that are waiting in the hereafter as promised by Allah. The earth is a paradise for disbelievers, since they attempt to take what they can of pleasure without regard to the limits imposed by Allah. They also sense the punishment that will be their eternal condition.

Children should appreciate that having the hereafter as a concern brings contentment and peace of mind. The Messenger of Allah (bpuh) said:

«Whoever has the hereafter as his main concern, Allah will fill his heart with a feeling of richness and independence; he will be focused and content, and this world will come to him in spite of itself. Whoever has this world as his main concern, Allah will cause him to feel constant fear of poverty; he will be distracted and unfocused, and he will have nothing of this world except what was already predestined for him.» (A sound hadith narrated by at-Tirmidhi and Aḥmad)

Death, in fact, may come at any moment and we need to be prepared at all times. We need to ready our children, for they may depart before us. Preparation is carried out by gaining knowledge, correcting beliefs, performing good deeds, and recalling the rewards that Allah has promised. The greatest reward will be Allah's pleasure and the opportunity to see Him and to be close to Him in the hereafter. What better reward for nurturing eemân?

{No disaster strikes upon the earth or among yourselves except that it is in a register [the Preserved Slate][39] before We bring it into being - indeed, that, for Allah, is easy. In order that you may not despair over what has eluded you and not exult [in pride] over what He has been given you...}

(Qur'an 57: 22-23)

Chapter Eleven:
Divine Will and Predestination

The Prophet (bpuh) said:

«Know that if the nation were to gather to benefit you with anything, it would benefit you only with something that Allah had already prescribed for you; if they gather to harm you with anything, they would harm you only with something Allah had already prescribed for you. The pens have been lifted and the pages have dried.» (A sound hadith narrated by at-Tirmidhi)

Belief in Divine Will and Predestination

Belief in predestination is the final pillar of eemân. There are many texts of the Qur'an that mention the will and decree of Allah. Allah has mentioned:

{Indeed, all things We created with predestination.}

(Qur'an 54: 49)

{...And ever is the command of Allah a destiny decreed.}

(Qur'an 33: 38)

{...[He] has created each thing and determined it with [precise] determination.}

(Qur'an 25: 2)

Many of the texts that mention the knowledge, power, will, and creation of Allah also refer to predestination. Belief in Allah's decree entails belief in all of these aspects.[40] Predestination is defined as decree, judgement, and ultimate destiny. Technically, it means:

> ...something of which there was prior knowledge, one of the things which was written by the Pen[41] when it wrote down everything that was going to happen for the rest of eternity, when Allah decreed the affairs of all His creation and what would happen before it happened. He knew that these things would happen at certain times that were known to Him, and in specific ways, and so things happen in the way that He has decreed.[42]

Ibn Ḥajar writes:

What is meant is that Allah knows how things will be and when they will happen, before He initiates them. Then He creates that which He already knows will happen. Hence everything that happens stems from His knowledge, power, and will.[43]

Belief in predestination is based upon four essential components:

1. Belief that the knowledge of Allah is all-encompassing:

    {...the Knower of the unseen. Not absent from Him is an atom's weight within the heavens or within the earth or [what is] smaller than that or greater, except that it is in a clear register.}

    (Qur'an 34: 3)

2. Belief that Allah has written everything that will happen until the Day of Resurrection (in the Preserved Slate):

    {Do you not know that Allah knows what is in the heaven and earth? Indeed, that is in a Record [the Preserved Slate]. Indeed that, for Allah, is easy.}

    (Qur'an 22: 70)

3. Belief in the will and perfect power of Allah - what He wills happens and what He does not will does not happen:

    {Verily, His command, when He intends a thing, is only that He says to it: Be! – and it is!}

    (Qur'an 36: 82)

4. Belief that Allah has created everything that exists, and that He has no partner in His creation:

    {Allah is the Creator of all things...}

    (Qur'an 39: 62)

{Indeed, all things We created with predestination.}

(Qur'an 54: 49)

Affirming each of these pillars leads to perfection of belief in predestination.[44] Ibn 'Abbâs said:

> Predestination is the essence of tawḥeed. Whoever worships Allah, the Almighty, alone and believes in predestination has perfected his tawḥeed, but whoever worships Allah alone but does not believe in predestination, destroys his tawḥeed by this disbelief.[45]

Connecting Children to Divine Will and Predestination

Belief in predestination revolves around the understanding that nothing happens in the world without Allah's knowledge, permission, and will. What Allah wills for a person will occur and what He does not will does not occur. No one can stop His decree or overpower His affairs. These are significant concepts for children to understand. Children should be trained to believe in predestination from a very young age and to accept the good and bad of it, for it is from Allah.

The Prophet (bpuh) taught 'Abdullâh ibn 'Abbâs about predestination while he was still a young boy. According to a hadith narrated by 'Abdullâh ibn 'Abbâs himself:

«One day I was behind the Prophet (bpuh) and he said to me: Young man, I shall teach you some words [of advice]: Be mindful of Allah, and Allah will protect you. Be mindful of Allah, and you will find Him in front of you. If you ask, ask Allah; if you seek help, seek help from Allah. Know that if the nation were to gather to benefit you with anything, it would benefit you only with something that Allah had already prescribed for you; if they gather to harm you with anything, they would harm you only with something Allah had already prescribed for you. The pens have been lifted and the pages have dried.» (A sound hadith narrated by at-Tirmidhi)[46]

In another version it reads:

«...Be mindful of Allah and you will find Him before you. Get to know Allah in prosperity and He will know you in adversity. Know that what has passed you by was not going to befall you; and that what has befallen you was not going to pass you by. Know that victory comes with patience, relief with affliction, and ease with hardship.» (A sound hadith narrated by at-Tirmidhi)[47]

A child who grows up with this understanding will have the strength and courage to face any and all challenges to his or her eemân. S/he will know that whatever s/he receives, s/he would never have missed; and that whatever s/he missed, s/he would never have received. S/he will comprehend that if all humans were to gather together to try and prevent something from happening, they would not be able to do so if Allah had already written it.

Likewise, if all humans were to gather to make something happen, they would not be able to do so if Allah had not willed it to occur.

This belief removes any fear or cowardice from the heart and replaces it with bravery and determination. The young person will live a life based upon the principles of Islam because s/he fears Allah and not other humans. S/he will defend Islam because s/he knows that what is destined for him or her is inevitable; s/he will stand up for his or her principles and practices even in the face of severe adversity. A young man who is ostracized for praying at school will not be bothered because he knows that he is on the path of truth and that they cannot harm him unless Allah wills. A young girl who is teased for wearing a hijab refuses to remove it for the same reasons. A person with belief in predestination will not bow down to any power on this earth because s/he knows that everything is in the hands of the Creator of the heavens and the earth and all that is between them.

When an event occurs about which they are displeased, they should be reminded that it only happened with Allah's will. Allah has a plan that humans may not understand and wisdom that they will never possess. Something that may seem very bad and negative to a person may, in essence, be very beneficial for them. Allah has reminded:

{But perhaps you hate a thing and it is good for you; and perhaps you love a thing and it is bad for you. And Allah knows, while you do not know.}

(Qur'an 2: 216)

Often, there are lessons in the events that transpire, and these should be discussed openly within the family. For example, sickness is an affliction for humans in this world, but it is beneficial for them in the hereafter since it is a way for forgiveness of sins and purification of the soul. When a child or someone close to him or her becomes ill, they can be reminded of this fact. This will assist them in accepting the illness and bearing it with patience in order to obtain the maximal benefits and blessings from Allah. The focus should be on the reward of being close to Allah as a result of the affliction. In a real example of such certainty in Allah's promise, one child in a Muslim family, in regard to her two siblings with Down syndrome, often used to say, "These are my doors to paradise."

Allah has mentioned:

{No disaster strikes except by permission of Allah. And whoever believes in Allah – He will guide his heart. And Allah is Knowing of all things.}

(Qur'an 64: 11)

The person who is suffering the calamity will know that it is from Allah and accept it and submit to it. Allah will guide his or her heart to certainty and serenity due to his or her belief in the decree of Allah. This will be true no matter how great the calamity. With this understanding, children will also be able to come to terms with the natural disasters that seem to be occurring at an increasing rate in our times.

The concepts of patience and gratitude should to be taught to children. They should learn to be patient during times of difficulty and tribulation, and grateful for Allah's blessings during times of ease. The Prophet (bpuh) said:

«The affair of the believer is amazing in that it is always good for him, and this is true only for a believer. If something joyful comes to him, he expresses gratitude and that is good for him. If something harmful comes to him, he is patient and that is good for him.» (Muslim)

Parents need to model these concepts themselves and remind their children to do the same.

Verses from the Qur'an may also be used to emphasize the importance of patience. Allah has reminded the believers repeatedly that they should seek help with patient perseverance.

{O you who have believed, seek help through patience and prayer. Indeed, Allah is with the patient.}

(Qur'an 2: 153)

{And We will surely test you with something of fear and hunger and a loss of wealth and lives and fruits, but give good tidings to the patient, who, when disaster strikes them, say: Indeed we belong to Allah, and indeed to Him we will return.}

(Qur'an 2: 155-156)

{...Indeed, the patient will be given their reward without limit.}

(Qur'an 39: 10)

Allah is with the one who patiently perseveres and He promises a great reward.

It would even be more beneficial for them to learn not only to be patient and forbearing, but to accept and be satisfied with Allah's decree and judgement. This is one of the highest levels of eemân that a human can attain. True patience is when we do not discriminate between a blessing and a severe trial, but welcome them both as a chance to earn great rewards from Allah, and to have an accepting attitude in all situations. Satisfaction comes from belief in predestination and that Allah has planned only the best for His believing slaves. Children should thus be reminded to be pleased with Allah's decree at all times.

It is important to make it clear to children that while Allah's will is present in the universe, humans still have the ability to choose either good or evil, submission or defiance. Allah would not judge us on the Day of Resurrection without this element of free will. Likewise, Allah will not hold a person accountable unless s/he has the ability to choose. For example, we are not accountable for things over which we have no control (height, place of birth, parents, and so forth). We are also not accountable unless we have the ability to reason and to make decisions. That is the reason that children and people with mental illness or mental retardation are not held responsible for their behaviours. Meeting or seeing someone with mental illness or retardation can offer opportunities for dialogue regarding these issues, particularly with older children and adolescents.

While Allah gave us a certain measure of free will, our will is dependent upon Allah's will. We cannot will anything, or accomplish it, unless and until Allah wills it! It should be clear to children that Allah's will is not arbitrary; rather there are wisdom, universal order and laws, and perfection in His plan.

Benefits of Believing in Predestination

Children should understand the benefits of believing in predestination. Belief in predestination brings peace of heart and mind and relief from grief, sadness and anger. There will only be tranquillity, happiness, certainty, and reassurance. This is due to the realization that everything that happens is according to Allah's divine decree and that there is a purpose and wisdom for everything that Allah does. There will be no need to despair, fret or give up hope. Other positive effects will transpire in the life of a person as well, such as motivation, confidence, success, and accomplishment. These are obvious goals that we have for our children.

Belief in predestination will also free the person from any form of *shirk* (associating partners with Allah) as s/he appreciates that Allah is the only one worthy of praying to, seeking assistance from, and relying upon. S/he will put his or her complete trust in and reliance upon Allah. All acts of worship will be directed toward the One who has decreed and determined all things. In this manner, tawḥeed is accurately and entirely fulfilled. The greatest result of belief in Allah's divine will and decree will be success in the hereafter.

Part III:
Developing an Islamic Personality in Children

One of the obvious purposes and goals of nurturing eemân in children is to develop an Islamic personality within them. An Islamic personality is one that submits completely to the will of Allah, as a servant of Allah. Through the process of submission, the soul becomes purified, which in turn affects the outward and inward characteristics of the individual. The actions, thoughts, and feelings reflect this Islamic personality, which is based upon the teachings in the Qur'an and in the Sunnah of the Prophet Muhammad (bpuh). The individual will act, think, and feel in the manner that Allah intended humans to act, think, and feel. Parents play an important role in this process and can either enhance or hinder the development of this Islamic personality. The following section sheds further light on this process and the tools that parents may utilize for the most beneficial outcome.

Chapter Twelve:

Additional Keys to Nurturing Eemân and Developing an Islamic Personality in Children

In addition to connecting children to the pillars of eemân, there are other strategies that parents may consider to nurture eemân and develop an Islamic personality and identity in their children. It will be helpful first to define a few terms for our purposes.

Definitions

Personality

Personality is the complex of characteristics that distinguishes an individual from others. It is the totality of an individual's emotional, behavioural and cognitive characteristics.

Identity

Identity is a comprehensive set of beliefs and practices that guide one's life. It provides a stable sense of self. A critical element in identity and identity formation is the belief system. The 'aqeedah of Islam imparts the necessary beliefs for a healthy and stable identity. Islamic law guides one's practices and behaviours.

Begin From an Early Age

The stories of a few Companions should be helpful in comprehending this point.

'Abdullâh ibn 'Abbâs

'Abdullâh ibn 'Abbâs was born three years before the migration to Madinah and he was only 13 years old when the Prophet (bpuh) died. As a young boy, he served the Prophet (bpuh), went with him on journeys and expeditions, and stood behind the Prophet (bpuh) in prayer.

He was like a shadow of the Prophet (bpuh), always in his company. The Prophet (bpuh) would often bring young 'Abdullâh close to him, pat him on the shoulder and pray:

«O Lord, make him acquire a deep understanding of the religion of Islam and instruct him in the meaning and interpretation of things.»[48] (Bukhari and Aḥmad)

His supplication was answered, for 'Abdullâh had wisdom beyond his years.[49]

Young 'Abdullâh was attentive to what the Prophet (bpuh) said and did in all situations. He listened and watched with an enthusiastic heart and committed the Prophet's (bpuh) words to memory. He became one of the most learned Companions of the Prophet (bpuh), memorizing 1,660 hadiths, many of which are recorded in Ṣaheeh al-Bukhâri and Ṣaheeh Muslim.[50] 'Abdullâh's life was to be devoted to the pursuit of learning and knowledge. He was also an ardent worshipper and a warrior, taking part in many battles.[51]

'Abdullâh ibn az-Zubayr

'Abdullâh ibn az-Zubayr was the son of az-Zubayr ibn al-'Awwâm, one of the ten Companions who were given the glad tidings of paradise. His mother was Asmâ' bint Abu Bakr, one of the first Muslims.

«When she migrated to Madinah, Asmâ' bint Abu Bakr was pregnant with 'Abdullâh ibn az-Zubayr. She arrived in Qubâ' and gave birth to 'Abdullâh there; then she sent him to Allah's Messenger (bpuh) so that he would rub the baby's palate with chewed dates…

He (the Holy Prophet) chewed them and then put his saliva in his mouth, so the first thing that entered his stomach was the saliva of Allah's Messenger (bpuh).

Asmâ' said: He then rubbed him and blessed him and gave him the name of 'Abdullâh.

'Abdullâh went to the Prophet (bpuh) when he was seven or eight years old, in order to pledge allegiance to Allah's Messenger (bpuh) as az-Zubayr had commanded him to do. Allah's Messenger (bpuh) smiled when he saw him coming towards him and then accepted his allegiance.» (Muslim)

'Abdullâh lived for long periods in the house of the Prophet (bpuh). This allowed him to live close to the Prophet (bpuh) and to absorb knowledge directly from the Messenger himself.[52]

'Abdullâh ibn az-Zubayr was bold and courageous even during his childhood. One day, 'Abdullâh was playing with his friends when the Caliph, 'Umar ibn al-Khaṭṭâb (May Allah be pleased with him), came towards them. The boys ran away quickly, for there was something awe-inspiring about 'Umar. 'Abdullâh, however, remained in his place and did not flee.

'Umar asked, "Why do you not flee with the (other) boys?"

'Abdullâh replied, "Commander of the Faithful, I have not committed any sin that I should run away from you, and the road is not narrow that I should make room for you."

'Umar said, "Indeed you are your father's son."

This boldness and courageousness was displayed on the battlefield as well. 'Abdullâh even took part in battles as a child. It is said that he attended the Battle of the Trench when he was only five years old, the battle against the Romans at the age of ten, and the Battle of Yarmook at the age of thirteen.[53] When the disbelievers ran away, he attacked them and started to kill their wounded. As a result of these experiences, he was strong and brave from childhood.

Lessons

The lesson from these stories of the two young 'Abdullâhs is that we should begin to nurture knowledge, eemân and piety in our children from a very young age. As mentioned previously, children should know about Allah from the moment of birth. As young children, time should be spent in memorization of the Qur'an and hadiths. It is interesting to note that psychological research has found that the ability to memorize information is strongest during the childhood years. As time goes on, this ability diminishes due to the processes of brain development and aging. The same is true of language acquisition, which is much easier during the childhood years.

The information that a child learns and memorizes during the formative years is likely to remain in the memory storage. Memorization of the Qur'an is especially important since it has positive effects upon the child's ability to memorize other material. Children who consistently memorize the Qur'an in childhood generally excel in other subjects as well. Young 'Abdullâh ibn 'Abbâs not only excelled in memorization of the Qur'an and hadiths, but he was a scholar in all respects. Parents should learn from this example and take advantage of the time that they have with their children.

The other issue to consider related to teaching children from a young age is that the main tasks of parenting take place during the early, formative years. Puberty and the age of responsibility emerge relatively early, sometimes as young as eight or nine years of age.

By this time, children should have the necessary and basic tools to manage, function, and make decisions as a responsible Muslim. Their behaviour should be commensurate with Islamic Law, for the angels will begin recording their deeds, both good and bad, to be presented on the Day of Judgement. For this reason, parents must begin early and prepare their children for this important time. The responsibility of parenting never really comes to an end, but the greatest effort should be exerted in the early phases. If this job is done well, the later years will run more smoothly.

Teach Children to Understand All Things from the Perspective of Islam

A person with an Islamic personality and strong eemân will look at all issues from the perspective of Islam. Islam becomes their criteria for right and wrong in all matters. One of the names of the Qur'an is the Criterion. It is the criterion between right and wrong, and for this reason it is the main source of knowledge for Muslims. It provides guidance for many areas of life and is further elaborated upon by the Hadith of the Prophet (bpuh).

Children should realize that all issues and situations should be viewed through the 'lens' of Islam, with the Qur'an and the Sunnah as the guides. Islam is a complete and comprehensive way of life that covers every aspect: spiritual, familial, social, economic, and political; as such, it can be applied to the various challenges and problems that one may face in life. A child, for example, may encounter a particularly difficult situation in school such as bullying or teasing by classmates. S/he should be encouraged to search in the Qur'an and the Hadith to find the most appropriate Islamic solution to his or her problem. What does the Qur'an say about dealing with others who act in a harmful way? What would the Prophet (bpuh) do in the same circumstances? Are there similar stories in the seerah to indicate how the Prophet (bpuh) may have coped with such tests? Through this process they not only learn about the Islamic approach to life, but they also gain a deeper understanding of the Qur'an and the Hadith as well.

Teach Importance of Obedience to Parents

The term that means 'obey' and related concepts appear many times in the Qur'an. Allah reminds us countless times to obey Him and to obey His Messenger. Allah has declared:

{Say: **Obey** Allah and **obey** the Messenger; but if you turn away – then upon him is only that [duty] with which he has been charged, and upon you is that with which you have been charged...}

(Qur'an 24: 54)

{So fear Allah as much as you are able and listen and obey and spend [in the way of Allah]; it is better for your souls. And whoever is protected from the stinginess of his soul – it is those who will be the successful.}

(Qur'an 64: 16)

As Muslims, we understand that obedience to Allah and to the Prophet (bpuh) is the path to true salvation. The Qur'an and the Sunnah of the Prophet (bpuh) are the integral components in this journey. There really is no other way. And oftentimes, to obey means to go against the wishes and desires of one's own soul, as mentioned in *Soorat at-Taghâbun* above, [whoever is protected from the stinginess of his soul]. As humans, we become prisoners of our desires unless and until we give allegiance to Allah. Obedience to Allah is the means through which all chains are broken and the soul is elevated. It is often a difficult struggle, but also a feasible achievement for each and every human being.

The importance of obedience can be seen in the rewards that are granted to those who submit and obey. Allah has mentioned:

{These are the limits [set by] Allah, and whoever obeys Allah and His Messenger will be admitted by Him to gardens [in Paradise] under which rivers flow, abiding eternally therein; and that is the great attainment.}

(Qur'an 4: 13)

What a beautiful recompense and a fitting abode: the gardens of paradise. Allah has also affirmed:

{And whoever obeys Allah and the Messenger – those will be with the ones upon whom Allah has bestowed favour of the prophets, the steadfast affirmers of truth, the martyrs and the righteous. And excellent are those as companions.}

(Qur'an 4: 69)

What more could one ask for? This is the promise of Allah.

Obedience in the Family Unit

We often forget that a condition somewhat comparable to that of paradise can also be attained in this life. Of course it will not be exactly the same, but there will be some similarities. In particular, we can achieve the serenity and joyfulness that is promised to the believers, as well as peacefulness, in realizing that Allah knows what is best for us. Within the family unit, synchrony and harmony can be achieved and love and respect can flourish. Again, this can only come about by following what Allah has ordained for optimal functioning of the family. Obedience is a major component of this formula.

For the family to function properly a wife needs to obey her husband and the children need to obey their parents (unless the husband or parents order them to be disobedient to Allah). When they do this, they are ultimately obeying Allah and receiving the greatest of rewards. Allah has described:

{...So righteous women are devoutly obedient, guarding in [the husband's] absence what Allah would have them guard...}

(Qur'an 4: 34)

In addition, a woman who obeys her husband provides the best role model for the children, to learn this righteous behaviour.

Children need to be taught this concept from a very young age, and the interactions between the mother and father provide ideal examples. The obedience of children to their parents is actually the training ground for eventual submission to Allah. In many ways they go hand in hand, but effective parenting provides the tangible examples that fit with the mind of a young child and ease the transition into responsibility. Notably, children must comprehend that obedience to parents is at the same time submission and obedience to Allah.

When a child learns obedience within the family unit, this generalizes into other areas of his or her life (in school, with peers, and with other adults). There are many situations in which we all need to listen and obey: student to teacher, worker to supervisor, soldier to commander, and so forth, with Allah as the final authority. Allah has commanded:

{O you who have believed, obey Allah and obey the Messenger and those in authority among you. And if you disagree over anything, refer it to Allah and the Messenger, if you should believe in Allah and the Last Day. That is the best [way] and best in result.} (Qur'an 4: 59)

This principle is necessary for optimal functioning of the society.

Part of the rationale behind this ruling is that parents and other adults have more experience than a child and consequently more wisdom. They have gained more knowledge, undergone more trials and tribulations, and learned from their own mistakes. It is important for children to understand that they have their best interests in mind when making decisions. This will assist the children in understanding the perspective of their parents and will build trust between them. Of course, Allah knows us better than we know our own selves, so He is our ultimate judge in all matters.

Encourage a Focus on Worthy Values and Related Projects

In this day and age, children spend a significant amount of time in useless and valueless pursuits. As parents of Muslim children, we need to focus on worthy values, goals, and projects, and instil the same aspirations in our children.

As we look at the situation of the world today, we see so much oppression, strife, destruction, and complete disregard for the fundamental rights of humans. Many of the victims of this death, devastation, and grief are Muslims. We must recall that it is our obligation to help our brothers, sisters and others who are suffering in the world today. Our Muslim brothers and sisters are calling out desperately for our help, and we must respond. We particularly need to take care of the children whose futures seem so dark and hopeless, and who are dependent upon adults for their needs.

The least that we can do is feel mercy and compassion for them. The Messenger of Allah (bpuh) said:

«You see the believers as regards their being merciful among themselves and showing love among themselves and being kind, resembling one body so that, if any part of the body is not well then the whole body shares the sleeplessness (insomnia) and fever with it.» (Bukhari)

We must make a supplication to Allah each day to relieve their hardship and suffering. We must act and do what is within our abilities to do. The Prophet (bpuh) said:

«Whoever observes something wrong should change it with his hands. If he is unable to do so, then he should speak against it with his tongue. If he is unable to do even that, then he should at least resent it in his heart – and this is the lowest level of faith.» (A sound hadith narrated by Ibn Mājah and at-Tirmidhī)

Teaching our Children

As parents, we not only need to fulfil our own obligation to the community, but we must also teach our children about the importance of worthy values such as charity, altruism, empathy, peace, and justice. Parents will find that feeling sympathy for others comes naturally to children. Children will innately want to help and give to others when they see them in need. We must firstly teach children about the condition of other Muslims and other people in the world.

They must know of the injustices, the oppression, the hunger, the poverty, and the anguish. They must realize the true nature of events. We should not protect them from the truth for fear of frightening them or worrying them. They must understand that it is only through Allah's mercy that they are not in the same situation as their Muslim brother or sister.

We then need to teach our children of the necessity of assisting those in need in any way possible. They must learn the true meaning of charity and its status in Islam. The Prophet (bpuh) said:

«Every small bone of everyone has a charity due upon it for every day upon which the sun rises. Bringing about justice between two is an act of charity. Helping a man get on his mount, lifting him onto it or helping him put his belongings on it, is a charity. A good word is a charity. Every step you take towards the prayer is a charity. And removing a harmful thing from the path is charity.» (Bukhari and Muslim)

The Prophet (bpuh) also said:

«Every Muslim has to give in charity. The people asked: O Allah's Prophet! If someone has nothing to give, what will he do? He said: He should work with his hands and benefit himself and also give in charity (from what he earns). The people further asked: If he cannot do even that? He replied: He should help the needy who appeal for help. Then the people asked: If he cannot do that? He replied: Then he should do all that is good and keep away from all that is evil, and this will be regarded as charitable deeds.» (Bukhari)

From these hadiths, we understand that charity goes beyond giving money alone and includes any good deed that benefits another human being. Children must learn this fundamental aspect of the religion and incorporate it into their lives from a very early age. Muslims should perform acts of charity on a daily basis and strive to benefit others through these acts. We particularly need to try and reach those who are most in need.

Children can collect and save money, clothing, and toys to be sent to those in need. They can participate in fundraising projects and activities to educate others about the suffering in the world. They can write letters and campaign against the injustices and oppression. The list of possibilities is endless. Through this process, the child begins to feel what it means to be a Muslim and to belong to the community. His or her eemân and Islamic personality will be strengthened immeasurably. His or her time will be spent in worthy pursuits and endeavours that will bring him or her rewards in this life and in the hereafter.

As time goes on, it becomes a part of the personality of the child to treat others with kindness and concern. S/he begins to realize the many wonderful blessings that s/he has received from Allah and s/he desires to demonstrate his or her gratefulness. In thankfulness to Allah, s/he uses the blessings that s/he has received (ability, wealth, health) to assist and improve those in need. S/he never misses any opportunity to perform an act of kindness because s/he realizes that no matter how much s/he performs, s/he can never match the wonderful blessings that s/he has received from Allah. What more could a parent desire for his or her child?

Teenagers, in particular, are idealists and have a fervent desire to change the world and make it a better place. Parents should encourage these natural desires and assist them in fulfilling their dreams and goals. There are many important causes and so much to be done. The keenness for volunteer work and social activism that a teenager participates in will undoubtedly be carried over into adulthood, so that the effort may continue. The inevitable outcome is the strengthening of the Muslim community and the achievement of its goals.

Be Good Role Models

As a starting point, parents must consistently engage in behaviour and speech that exemplifies the true nature of being Muslim. Children derive many of their ideas about roles and values from significant individuals with whom they interact and have close relationships. Of course, the parents would be the main figures in this process as discussed elsewhere. Young people are generally drawn to the values and attitudes of a special person—a parent, an admired teacher, an older sibling, or a famous person—whose ideas and behaviours the youth admires. Adults should give young people reasons to admire them and strive to be successful role models, mentors, and guides. The values, attitudes, and behaviour that youth learn from these significant others will be integrated into their Islamic personality and identity.

Of course, the greatest role model for the whole Muslim community is Prophet Muhammad (bpuh). We have his model available to us in writing and it can be brought to life in our own behaviour. We cannot expect our children to live and behave in a certain manner if we are not doing it ourselves. The opportunity to influence children is readily awaiting; we just need to take advantage of it.

Demonstrate and Encourage Pride in Being Muslim

Parents should take the lead in demonstrating pride in the religion of Islam and in being Muslim. Children are very perceptive and can sense the feelings and thoughts of their parents, even if they do not readily show in behaviour. Pride, in this context, is very different from arrogance in that it refers to a sense of dignity and certainty, and a commitment to carry the banner of Islam for the sake of Allah. Muslims should be proud of the gift that they have been given from Allah and should work to spread it wherever they are. Pride, self-respect, and self-esteem are key components of identity and facilitate the stable and consistent sense of who we are and how we fit into society. If self-esteem does not come from being Muslim, a person will attempt to gain it through other means. Children and youth are particularly vulnerable as these aspects develop gradually during those years.

Teach the true meaning of 'Jihad'

Jihad is one of the mainstays of Islam that has been abandoned by the majority of the Muslim community. This is one of the causes of the humiliation of Muslims in our time. The grief and suffering caused by current circumstances is overwhelming. As Muslims, we know that the only viable solution is returning to the Qur'an and the Sunnah. Principles of justice, security, and honour can only be guaranteed fully with the implementation of Allah's laws on the earth, which deserve the utmost respect and honour. The ultimate goal in the struggle is to establish Islam, in order to eliminate all forms of oppression completely and give Allah the devotion and adoration that only He deserves.

This is a process that does not come easily, as it requires a great struggle. This struggle, in the Islamic sense, is termed jihad. Jihad is an Arabic term that means to strive, struggle, and work to improve, and it can be applied to any effort exerted by a person. In an Islamic sense, the general meaning of jihad is to strive in the path of Allah or for the cause if Allah.

Its goal is to establish the religion of Islam in our hearts, in our homes, in our communities, and in our countries. Allah has indicated in the Qur'an:

{And those who strive for Us–We will surely guide them to Our ways. And indeed, Allah is with the doers of good.} (Qur'an 29: 69)

{The believers are only the ones who have believed in Allah and His Messenger and then doubt not, but strive with their properties and their lives in the cause of Allah. It is those who are the truthful.} (Qur'an 49: 15)

Jihad means to struggle against injustice, oppression, corruption, tyranny, exploitation, and the denial of basic human rights. It means to fight against sacrilege and blasphemy of Allah, His Messenger (bpuh), and His Book. It means to strive against the enemies of Islam, both visible and unseen, for Satan has an army working with him. Allah has specified:

{Those who believe fight in the cause of Allah, and those who disbelieve fight in the cause of false objects of worship. So fight against the allies of Satan. Indeed, the plot of Satan has ever been weak.}

(Qur'an 4: 76)

Ultimately, jihad is the struggle against Satan and his assistants, who appear in the form of jinn and humans.

Jihad is an essential element in the religion of Islam, and to realize what occurs when it is abandoned means to understand its status; for without jihad, evil will reign. Jihad is so significant that those who perform it are regarded as the best of people. Abu Sa'eed Al-Khudri narrated:

«Somebody asked: O Allah's Messenger! Who is the best among the people?

Allah's Messenger (bpuh) replied: A believer who strives his utmost in Allah's cause with his life and property.» (Bukhari)

The Prophet (bpuh) has described jihad as better than anything in the world. He said:

«To go forth in the morning or evening to fight in the path of Allah is better than the whole world and everything in it.» (Muslim)

To comprehend the profoundness of this statement is to grasp the true nature of sacrifice, fear of Allah, and spirituality in Islam.

Jihad has also been associated with performance of prayers and being kind to parents, two of the fundamentals of the faith.

«A man asked the Prophet (bpuh): What deeds are the best?

The Prophet replied: To perform the (daily compulsory) prayers at their (early) stated fixed times, to be good and dutiful to one's parents, and to participate in jihad in Allah's cause.» (Bukhari)

In another hadith, its status has been elevated above other acts of worship.

«A man said: O Allah's Messenger! Inform me of an act that is equal to jihad (in Allah's cause)!

Allah's Messenger (bpuh) responded: You cannot (do that act).

The man insisted: Tell me what it is.

Allah's Messenger (bpuh) asked: Can you fast continuously without eating or drinking (at all) and stand continuously in prayer from the time the warriors go out for jihad (till the time they return back home)?

The man replied: No.

Allah's Messenger said: That is (the act) which is equal to jihad.» (Bukhari and Muslim)

The Prophet (bpuh) himself loved jihad and wished for martyrdom. Narrated Abu Hurayrah:

«I heard Allah's Messenger (bpuh) saying: By Him in Whose Hands my soul is! Were it not for some men amongst the believers who dislike to be left behind me, and whom I cannot provide with means of conveyance, I would certainly never remain behind any army unit going out for jihad in Allah's cause. By Him in Whose Hands my life is! I would love to be martyred in Allah's cause and then come back to life and then be martyred and then come back to life again and then be martyred and then come back to life again and then be martyred.» (Bukhari)

Few elements of the faith parallel jihad in status and honour. It is an integral component of Islam as it is a struggle for Allah and His religion. The striving is, in actuality, for the human being himself or herself, as this path leads to nearness to Allah, contentment of the soul, and the eventual goal of paradise in the hereafter. For this reason, some of the Companions used to take their children to the battlefield to teach them bravery and to instil in them a desire for jihad.

These are the messages that we should give to our children regarding the status and importance of jihad.

Talk to Them about the Heroes of Earlier Generations, Islamic Battles and Victories

Talking to children about heroes in Islam and about Muslim victories will encourage them to be brave and courageous. This is an important part of being powerful and honourable, and developing a willingness to struggle against evil in all forms of jihad. Children are eager to have role models and they love to hear stories of heroism and bravery. This is particularly true for young boys. Their heroes should be the Companions and warriors who struggled for the sake of Allah.

Their battlefields should be those of Islam against disbelief. They should be exposed to stories of brave companions who sacrificed their lives for the sake of Allah, the leaders of Muslim armies at various times throughout history, and the legendary Muslim scholars who struggled against injustice. They should be familiar with the history of Islam, the battles that occurred, and the victories that were achieved through the assistance of Allah.

Place Islam before Ethnicity and Nationality

Two major threats to the development of a Muslim identity are ethnicity and nationality. Allah actually warns about this several times in the Qur'an. He has mentioned:

{And when it is said to them: Follow what Allah has revealed, they say: Rather, we will follow that which we found our fathers doing. Even though their fathers understood nothing, nor were they guided?}

(Qur'an 2: 170)

This has happened throughout history and it continues to this day. Many Muslims today place greater emphasis on their cultural traditions and nationality than they do on Islamic values and practices. This means that their national and ethnic identities are much stronger than their Islamic identity. Evidence of this is shown in the fact that mosques are often divided along ethnic or national lines and social groups are formed based upon these factors. A more frightening occurrence is to see people reject a matter in the Qur'an or the Hadith on some aspect because their family has "always done it another way" and they do not want to change.

Often, the culture and traditions of the ethnic group are confused with Islam. Practices that are purely cultural may be attributed to Islam and vice versa.

Children should be taught that Muslim identity and Islam come before all else. Muslims are brothers and sisters to one another regardless of race, ethnicity, or nationality; and there is no superiority of one over the other in any of these. They must also understand that there is nothing more important than being a Muslim. There is grave danger in placing ethnicity or nationality above Islam as it may actually lead to various forms of misguidance and shirk. Of course, there is also the danger of the dominant culture for those living in the West. Although Islam accepts and recognizes the value and beauty of the variety of cultures, traditions, and languages, religion should be given priority when it comes to relevant matters.

Chapter Thirteen:
Enhancing the Islamic Personality and Building Self-Esteem

«Allah will show no mercy to those who do not show mercy to others.»[54]

There are additional steps that can be taken to enhance the Islamic personality and identity of children as well as build strong self-esteem and confidence. These suggestions are discussed below with an emphasis on self-esteem.

Definitions of Self-Concept and Self-Esteem

Self-concept is a mental image of one's self. It is comprised of terms that a person uses to describe himself or herself. Such terms may include outgoing, shy, curious, brave, intelligent, and so forth.

Self-esteem is the evaluation of information contained in a person's self-concept. It is considered to be the level of confidence and satisfaction in one's self. A person with high self-esteem feels confident and pleased with his or her concept or idea of himself or herself.

Importance of Self-Esteem

Research has found that children who are morally and spiritually conscious develop a sense of their own self-worth. Parents can assist children in developing an Islamic personality and high self-esteem. Self-esteem is an important factor in social and emotional adjustment. Children with high self-esteem are more capable of making good decisions, are proud of their accomplishments, are willing to take responsibility, and act independently. They are better able to cope with stressful situations and are enthusiastic about challenges. They also have the ability to handle positive and negative emotions and are more socially competent.

Building Self-Esteem

Nurture the Special Gifts from Allah

Each child is born with unique personality traits, temperaments, skills, abilities, and special gifts from Allah. These gifts were given to a child for a purpose. They should be nurtured and allowed to develop to their fullest capacity. Children should be taught to dedicate their talents and resources to Allah's service. This gives value, purpose and direction in life. Parents play an important role in this regard. They first need to determine the special characteristics and gifts of each child and then find ways to enhance them. If a child's natural abilities are not allowed to grow, this may negatively affect self-esteem.

Love Your Children Abundantly

Parents should show their children how much they care for and love them. They should tell their children on a regular basis that they love them. Children should also be treated with respect and courtesy since actions often speak louder than words. Physical contact is essential, including such things as hugs, kisses, strokes, pats on the back. An important aspect also is that parents should spend time with their children whenever possible. This may involve playing games, talking, taking a walk, praying and reading the Qur'an together, going to the mosque, or sharing other favourite activities. A sense of humour also goes a long way in dealing with many situations and for strengthening the parent-child relationship.

In the example of Prophet Muhammad (bpuh), we find someone who was always kind, respectful, and affectionate toward children. The Prophet (bpuh) loved children a great deal. He would offer greetings to children when he met them in the street and he would play and joke with them. He would allow his grandsons, al-Ḥasan and al-Ḥusayn, to ride on his shoulders and would hug and kiss them openly. Ya'lâ ibn Murrah mentioned:

«We went out with the Prophet (bpuh) and we were called to eat, when we saw al-Ḥusayn playing in the street. The Prophet rushed ahead of the people, holding out his arms, and the child was running here and there; the Prophet was laughing with him until he caught him, then he put one of the child's hands under his chin and the other on top of his head, and embraced him.» (Bukhari)

The Prophet (bpuh) used physical affection toward all children. Usâmah ibn Zayd said:

«Allah's Messenger (bpuh) used to put me on (one of) his thighs and put al-Ḥasan ibn 'Ali on his other thigh, and then embrace us and say: O Allah! Please be merciful to them, as I am merciful to them.» (Bukhari)

Yoosuf ibn 'Abdus-Salâm said:

«The Prophet of Allah (bpuh) named me Yoosuf, sat me on his knee, and stroked my head.» (Bukhari, Aḥmad and At-Tirmidhi)

In a well-known hadith, Abu Hurayrah narrated:

«The Prophet of Allah (bpuh) kissed al-Ḥasan ibn 'Ali while Aqra' ibn Ḥâbis was sitting nearby.

Aqra' said: I have ten children and have never kissed any of them.

The Prophet (bpuh) looked at him and said: Those who show no mercy will be shown no mercy.» (Bukhari and Muslim)

'Â'ishah (*Raḍiya Allâhu 'Anhâ* – May Allah be pleased with her) reported:

«A Bedouin came to the Prophet (bpuh) and said: You (people) kiss your children! We don't kiss ours.

The Prophet (bpuh) said: I cannot put mercy in your heart after Allah has removed it.» (Bukhari, Muslim and Ibn Mâjah)

Communicate With Your Children

In the US, the average American child spends 1,680 minutes per week in front of a machine (TV) and only 38.5 minutes in a meaningful conversation with his or her parents. Some young people spend more time on the computer communicating with people half-way around the world than they spend talking with their parents in the next room. It is very important that parents communicate with their children EVERY DAY, not only for self-esteem enhancement, but for many other reasons as well.

It is very difficult to build a relationship with any human being without frequent communication. Communication is what relationships are based upon. This is definitely true for the parent-child relationship as well. We cannot expect to have an influence upon our children unless we have regular contact with them.

This is particularly true as the child gets older and begins to understand more about the world. If the lines of communication are open, it is more likely that s/he will come to his or her parents to find answers to important questions that come up in life. This offers unique opportunities for parents to share their beliefs and values in a direct and real way. Without a history of open communication, this may never happen. A line of communication is also essential for effective discipline.

The most critical element for effective communication is listening (really listening). This means giving your child undivided attention, putting aside your feelings and opinions for a moment, and trying to understand those of your child. His or her ideas, emotions, and feelings should be taken seriously. Parents should show their children that what they do is important by talking with them about their activities and interests. At times, it may be necessary to express values and beliefs, but this should be done in a calm manner and accompanied with a rationale. Problems should be discussed without placing blame or commenting on a child's character.

Praise Them for Good Behaviour

Children respond well to praise and positive attention and this can go a long way in preventing problem behaviours and reducing them once they occur. The use of such phrases or remarks also builds self-esteem. Examples include, "Thank you for helping", "That was an excellent idea!", "You are terrific!", "What a nice job!", "*Mâ shâ' Allâh!*",[55] and "Allah will be pleased with you." Praise, recognition, special privileges, or increased responsibility may be given for accomplishments and successes. Hugs and kisses may be used as rewards as well.

Praise and kindness are much more effective as forms of discipline than harshness and physical punishment. In effect, they act as preventive tools. The Prophet (bpuh) said:

«When Allah wills some good towards the people of a household, He introduces kindness among them.» (A sound hadith recorded by Aḥmad)

The Prophet (bpuh) also said:

«Allah loves kindness and rewards it in such a way that he does not reward for harshness or for anything else.» (Muslim)

Children who are treated with respect and kindness respond more easily and quickly to the disciplinary efforts of parents. This prevents many arguments and confrontations.

Give Them Praise and Respect in Front of Others

«Sahl ibn Sa'd said that the Prophet (bpuh) was brought a cup and he drank from it. There was a boy, the youngest of all the people, on his right and some elders on his left.

He asked: Child, will you allow me to give this to these elders?

The boy replied: I will not give away my share of your blessings to anyone, O Messenger of Allah.

Thus, the Prophet (bpuh) gave the cup to the boy.» (Bukhari)[56]

This hadith provides a unique and valuable example of respect for children. It is likely that most adults in that same situation would ignore the child or ask him or her to go away so as not to bother the grown-ups. It seems odd that some parents show a great deal of respect to perfect strangers but fall short when it comes to their own children. The Prophet (bpuh) demonstrated the proper manner of dealing with such a situation. Children are human beings and they deserve the same level of respect as any other human being. It is important to respect and admire our children at all times, particularly in front of other people. This sends a very powerful message that a parent values his or her children and considers them to be a worthy member of the community. The Prophet (bpuh) often included young children and youth in study circles with other Companions. These types of experiences are invaluable for character development and lead to a smooth transition into adulthood and the responsibilities of life.

Avoid Humiliating or Shaming Them

Parents should avoid humiliating or shaming children, particularly in the presence of others. Their ideas should not be belittled nor should they be ridiculed or ostracized. Anas narrated:

«I served the Prophet (bpuh) for ten years, and he never said to me: Uff – and never blamed me by saying: Why did you do that or why did you not do that?» (Bukhari)

This is another compelling illustration of kind treatment toward children; ten years and not one instance of impatience or negative commentary. Some parents are with their children for five minutes and find some way to blame them for every bad thing that happened that day.

Humiliation, shame, and ridicule only serve to harm a child's personality and well-being. In essence, they have the opposite effect of praise and kindness. They lead to a decrease in self-esteem and self-confidence and, in severe cases, a disturbed personality and behaviour problems.

We can imagine how we feel when someone gives us a negative comment or humiliates us in some way.

It can be hurtful and embarrassing. Children feel the same way and, due to the fact that their personalities and characters are developing, they are much more vulnerable than adults. As a result, they are more likely to suffer from the harmful effects of such actions and carry these effects with them for longer periods of time. Parents should constantly be aware of the sensitive nature of children and their unique vulnerability.

Consult Them and Ask for Their Opinions

Consulting children about certain matters helps them to feel grown-up, responsible, and trustworthy. They feel that their opinions are valued when they are asked to express their point of view. It also strengthens their sense of belonging and responsibility toward the family unit. The amount and type of consultation that is done depends, of course, on the age and developmental level of each child. As children reach the teenage years, it becomes even more important to involve them in family discussions. This approach enhances the skills that will be invaluable for them in adult life, such as communication skills, problem-solving, decision-making, compromise, and so forth.

It would be advisable to arrange and conduct family meetings to discuss issues related to the family and its members. A family meeting is basically a structured discussion time that typically is scheduled on a regular basis and involves all members of a family. It provides a forum for making group decisions, assigning responsibilities, sharing positive feelings, and choosing activities for family fun. Problems that family members are facing may be discussed along with possible solutions. These meetings will assist in establishing strong ties, interaction, and cooperation amongst family members. It should be clear, however, that with any form of consultation or family meetings the final authority and decision-making rests with the parents due to their position within the family.

Foster Responsibility and Independence

Children should be given responsibilities according to their age and abilities. This provides training for the development of conscientious, trustworthy, and independent behaviour. As young adults, they will eventually need to make their own important decisions in their lives. With appropriate experience, they are provided with opportunities to learn and develop essential decision-making and problem-solving skills.

They should then be encouraged to apply these skills on a regular basis. As children get older, they should gradually be allowed more freedom and control over their lives, within suitable limits. Parents should continue to provide support when necessary. The development of responsibility and independence is key to anyone's self-confidence and high self-esteem. Such a child will feel valued, appreciated, and competent. This, in turn, will increase the level of trust between a parent and child and enhance the parent-child relationship, which is so vital in achieving the goals that have been set.

Part IV:

Environmental Factors

The environment surrounding children may also have an impact upon their spiritual development. This influence is often subtle, but nonetheless can be quite significant. This is particularly true as the child matures and moves from childhood into adolescence and early adulthood. The general understanding in the field of development is that as a child develops, the influence of parents tends to diminish (although it never ends) and the role of peers and the community becomes more significant. It is a gradual process, which of course will vary from person to person. The good news is that in most cases, youth tend to eventually integrate the morals and values of their parents, even if they spend a period of time 'testing the limits'. Regardless of this encouraging fact, it is important to monitor the home environment itself; the peer environment (their friends, their activities, and so forth); and the community environment, to ensure the most spiritually enriching experiences for your child.

Chapter Fourteen:
The Home Environment

Home is a sanctuary and a blessing from Allah. Allah has mentioned:

{And Allah has made for you from your homes a place of rest…}

(Qur'an 16: 80)

It is the peaceful haven to which people retreat from the hardships of this life. Shelter, protection, privacy and enjoyment are found within this enclosure.

Home is also the base for developing and nurturing children with eemân. Children acquire most of their values, beliefs, and behaviours from interactions within this environment. Understanding the responsibility and influence of parenting, parents should ensure that the home offers an environment in which eemân may grow and flourish. This can be accomplished by following a few useful guidelines, centred around instituting that which is good and beneficial and removing that which causes evil or harm.

Create an Environment of *Eemân* Within the Home

The Prophet (bpuh) said:

«The comparison between a home in which Allah is remembered and a home in which Allah is not remembered is like comparing the living and the dead.» (Muslim)

The home must be a place where Allah is remembered throughout the day through prayer, reading the Qur'an, remembrance of Allah, supplication, discussion of Islamic topics, reading Islamic books, and so on. These are things that should occur on a consistent basis so that the angels will enter the home and bring Allah's blessings.

Reading the Qur'an should be a regular activity of the members of the household. It is particularly beneficial to recite *Soorat al-Baqarah* (Chapter Two of the Qur'an – The Cow) on a regular basis to protect the home from the workings of Satan. Allah's Messenger (bpuh) said:

«Do not make your houses into graves. Satan flees from a house in which Soorat al-Baqarah is recited.» (Muslim)

The Prophet (bpuh) also said:

«Recite Soorat al-Baqarah in your homes, for Satan does not enter a home in which Soorat al-Baqarah is recited.» (Muslim)

The last two verses of this chapter contain special virtues. The Prophet (bpuh) said:

«Allah wrote a document two thousand years before He created the heavens and the earth, which is kept near the Throne, and He revealed two verses of it with which He concluded Soorat al-Baqarah. If they are recited in a house for three consecutive nights, Satan will not approach it.» (A reliable hadith recorded by at-Tirmidhi)

Establish Prayer within the Home

Prayer should be established within the home at its required time, and members of the family should pray in congregation when several are present. Establishment of prayer means not only to fulfil the prayer, but to complete it on time and with humbleness. The family may also designate a specific area for prayer and maintain its uniqueness and cleanliness. For women, it is better to pray each prayer within the home. For men, it is recommended to pray voluntary prayers at home before or after having prayed obligatory prayers in the mosque. The Prophet (bpuh) said:

«The voluntary prayer in the home is better than the voluntary prayer with the people. It is like the obligatory prayer of the man in congregation being better than praying the obligatory by himself.» (Bukhari)

The Prophet (bpuh) also said:

«When any one of you observes prayer in the mosque he should reserve a part of his prayer for his home, for Allah would make the prayer as a means of betterment in his home.» (Muslim)

This is to ensure that homes are made places of worship just as the mosques. In one story related to this issue:

«'Utbân ibn Mâlik, (one of the Companions of the Prophet [bpuh]) came to the Messenger of Allah (bpuh) and said: I am losing my eyesight, and I lead the prayer. When it rains, the riverbed between me and them gets flooded and I cannot get to their mosque to lead them in prayer. O Messenger of Allah, I would like you to come and pray in my house so that I can take it as a place of prayer.

The Messenger of Allah (bpuh) said: I will do that, inshallah (God willing).

'Utbân said: The next day the Messenger of Allah and Abu Bakr came in the morning. The Messenger of Allah asked permission to enter, and I gave him permission. He did not sit down until he entered the house, then he said: Where would you like me to pray in your house?

I showed him a corner of the house, then the Messenger of Allah stood up, said: Allâhu akbar; we stood in a row behind him, and he prayed two units of prayer and gave the *tasleem*[57] at the end of the prayer.» (Bukhari)

The members of the household should encourage and remind one another regarding the prayer. 'Â'ishah (May Allah be pleased with him) said:

«The Messenger of Allah (bpuh) used to pray at night, and when he prayed *witr*[58] he would say: Get up and pray witr, 'Â'ishah.» (Muslim)

The Prophet (bpuh) said:

«May Allah have mercy on a man who gets up at night and prays, then he wakes up his wife to pray, and if she refuses he throws water in her face.» (Recorded by Aḥmad with a sound chain)

These principles can also be applied to children, particularly as they reach the age of learning their prayers.

Make Teaching and Learning Ongoing Activities

Teaching and learning should be ongoing activities in every Muslim household. Attaining knowledge regarding the religion is incumbent upon all members of the family and is the basis upon which eemân will flourish. The head of the household has the primary responsibility to ensure that he is guiding his family to the correct path, enjoining them to do what is good and right, and forbidding them from wrongdoing. Both father and mother work together to teach the children correct Islamic 'aqeedah, the pillars of Islam, the pillars of eemân, what Allah has enjoined, what He has prohibited, and Qur'anic memorization. A study circle should be established within the home that covers these various topics, and from which all family members will benefit. Children should especially be encouraged to participate since this will establish a pattern for them that will be carried throughout their lifetimes. As they become older, they may even be requested to prepare topics for presentation.

Other sources of learning may be scholarly lectures, recitation of the Qur'an, or Islamic stories. The possibilities for acquiring knowledge are endless.

Maintain an Islamic Library

Each home should have its own small Islamic library. This may include such things as books, cassette tapes, CDs, and videos. It is important to choose accurate and reliable material that adheres to the Sunnah. There should be a variety of materials to cover the needs of all age levels and languages of those in the home. Arabic material is definitely a must since everyone in the family should either know or be learning to read the language of the Qur'an. Books should cover a variety of topics, be properly organized, and be easily accessible. Audiotapes and CDs may include Qur'anic recitation, lectures, children's tapes containing supplications, reminders of Islamic manners, and religious songs with no musical instruments. Family members should encourage one another to use these materials on a regular basis, and they should be shared with other Muslim families who may be in need of them.

Know the Supplications and Islamic Rulings that Pertain to Houses

Members of the household should remember Allah and say "bismillâh" when entering the home. The Messenger of Allah (bpuh) said:

«When any one of you enters his home and mentions the name of Allah when he enters and when he eats, Satan says: You have no place to stay and nothing to eat here. If he enters and does not mention the name of Allah when he enters, Satan says: You have a place to stay. If he does not mention the name of Allah when he eats, Satan says: You have a place to stay and something to eat.» (Muslim and Aḥmad)

The specific supplication for entering the home is the following:

«In the name of Allah we enter and in the name of Allah we leave, and in our Lord we place our trust. [*Bismillâhi walajnâ, wa bismillâhi kharajnâ, wa 'alâ Rabbinâ tawakkalnâ.*]»[59] (An acceptable hadith recorded by Abu Dâwood; according to al-Albâni, its chain of narration is broken, while Ibn Bâz graded the same is reliable).

There is also supplication when leaving the home. The Prophet (bpuh) said:

«If a person goes out of his house and says: In the name of Allah, I put my trust in Allah, there is no help and no strength except in Allah [*Bismillâhi, tawakkaltu 'alâ Allâh, wa lâ ḥawla wa lâ quwwata illâ billâh*], it will be said to him: This will take care of you, you are guided, you have what you need and you are protected. Satan will stay away from him, and another devil will say to him: What can you do with a person who is guided, provided for and protected?» (A sound hadith recorded by Abu Dâwood and at-Tirmidhi)

Some of the Islamic rulings regarding homes include guarding the secrets of the home, seeking permission to enter, not looking into other people's homes, and not allowing children to enter the parent's bedroom during certain times of the day. Regarding seeking permission to enter, Allah has informed us:

{O you who have believed, do not enter houses other than your own houses until you ascertain welcome and greet their inhabitants. That is best for you; perhaps you will be reminded. And if you do not find anyone therein, do not enter them until permission has been given you. And if it is said to you: Go back, then go back; it is purer for you. And Allah is Knowing of what you do.}
(Qur'an 24: 27-28)

It is prohibited to look into the homes of other people without their permission. The Messenger of Allah (bpuh) said:

«If someone looks into a person's house without their permission, put his eye out, and there is no compensation payment or legal retribution in this case.» (A sound hadith recorded by Aḥmad)

In another hadith, it is narrated:

«A man peeped through a hole in the door of the Messenger's house, and at that time, the Messenger (bpuh) had an iron comb with which he was combing his hair. So when the Messenger (bpuh) saw him, he said (to him): If I had been sure that you were looking at me (through the door), I would have poked your eye with this (sharp iron comb).

The Prophet (bpuh) added: Asking for permission to enter has been made obligatory so that one may not look unlawfully (at what there is in the house without the permission of its inhabitants).» (Bukhari)

Children should be informed that there are certain times of the day that they must seek permission to enter their parents' bedroom. These times are before the dawn prayer, at nap time, and after the evening prayer. Allah has mentioned:

{O you who have believed, let those whom your right hands possess and those who have not [yet] reached puberty among you ask permission of you [before entering] at three times: before the dawn prayer, when you put aside your clothing [for rest] at noon, and after the night prayer. [These are] three times of privacy for you. There is no blame upon you nor upon them beyond these [periods], for they circulate continually among you – some of you, among others. Thus does Allah make clear to you the verses [His ordinances]; and Allah is Knowing and Wise.}

(Qur'an 24: 58)

The privacy of personal affairs is highly respected in Islam as reflected in the above rulings. Care should be taken to preserve this virtue within the home. In addition, when visitors are present, men and women should sit in separate areas. There should be no mixing of men and women, since this can lead to temptation and uncomfortable or awkward situations. This should be applied regardless of whether the visitors are Muslims or non-Muslims. The rules are for your home and they should be respected by those who enter.

Invite Righteous and Knowledgeable People to the Home

Allah has mentioned:

{My Lord, forgive me and my parents and whoever enters my house as a believer, and the believing men and believing women…}

(Qur'an 71: 28)

Righteous people who enter your home will bring many benefits due to their presence and to conversations with them. They are more likely to discuss useful topics and may be excellent sources of information and knowledge. We should always pray that Allah will bless us with righteous friends, since they can have such positive effects on us. The Prophet (bpuh) said:

«Keep company with a believer only, and let your food be eaten only by the righteous.» (A reliable hadith narrated by Abu Dâwood and at-Tirmidhi)

Remove Negative Influences from the Home

Negative influences should be removed from the home, including, statues, and pictures of animate beings. Each of these is discussed in more detail below.

Unlawful Music

{And among people is he who buys the amusement of speech to mislead [others] from the way of Allah without knowledge and who takes it [Allah's way] in ridicule. Those will have a humiliating punishment.}

(Qur'an 31: 6)

The explanation for "amusement of speech" is that which has no benefit, including misleading stories and frivolous songs or music. In general, it includes all that distracts or diverts one from the Qur'an and the remembrance of Allah.

It is permissible, however, to listen to Islamic songs that include wisdom, exhortation, encouragement to do good, and promotion of noble attitudes and characteristics. This is particularly true if the songs revive Islamic thoughts and feelings, and motivate the listener to obey Allah by living within the framework of Islamic Law, to avoid transgressing the limits set by Allah, and to strive in jihad for His sake. The most appropriate times for Islamic songs include during Eid,[60] weddings, when travelling for jihad, or when feeling bored and in need of something to revive spirits. This should not be regarded as something that must be adhered to or a habit engaged in on a continual basis.

Pictures, Statues

A Muslim home should be free of pictures with animate beings, statues, so that angels will enter. The Prophet (bpuh) said:

«Angels (of mercy) do not enter a house wherein there is an image of a living creature (a human being or an animal).» (Bukhari)

This ruling for pictures applies to images of animate beings, while inanimate objects are allowed. The reason for the prohibition is that picture-making involves imitating the creative act of Allah. The Messenger of Allah (bpuh) said:

«The people who will receive the severest punishment on the Day of Resurrection will be those who try to make likenesses of Allah's creations.» (Bukhari)

He also said:

«Those who make these pictures will be punished on the Day of Resurrection, and it will be said to them: Bring to life what you have created.» (Bukhari)

Since picture-making of animate beings is prohibited, it is also forbidden to buy, sell, or display them. The same ruling obviously applies to statues of animate beings. Some scholars also conclude that photographs of humans or animals are prohibited as well.

Ensure that Physical Aspects are Conducive to Fulfilling Religious Obligations

It is preferable for the home to be close to a mosque so that it will be easier for men to attend the prayers in congregation and for all family members to visit the mosque for lectures, study groups, and social gatherings. In order to obtain the benefits of community, it is also advisable to find an area where other Muslims live. One should definitely be careful about close neighbours and avoid those who are obviously engaged in immoral activity. When choosing a house or apartment, consideration should be made regarding privacy and the availability of separate sitting areas for men and women. Additionally, although most scholars agree that it is permissible to face the qibla while relieving oneself inside buildings or places where there is a screen between oneself and the Kaaba, it is best to ensure that toilets are situated in such a way as to avoid facing the direction of the *qibla*.[61] The house should be spacious and fulfil safety and health requirements.

Dangers for the Soul

The dangers of friends that are not Muslims. The most obvious is the diversion from worship and remembrance of Allah. Through its entrance into the mind and heart of the child, some friends have the capability to cause serious damage to the soul. A person who spends a great deal of with people that are not Muslims is less likely to pray on time (if at all) or to join the congregational prayer. Staying up late for viewing causes the person to miss the dawn prayer. There is little time for reading of Qur'an, and so on.

In addition to the time that is lost to meaningless pursuits, there is also exposure to countless un-Islamic values and practices. Most of these are very obvious, while others are more subtle. Some of the more obvious include social mixing between males and females, inappropriate dress, aggressive and unacceptable social behaviour, lack of respect for authority, celebrating of non-Muslim holidays, and so on.

For children, the real threat lies in the fact that these values begin to be internalized and become a part of the personality structure. Children begin to assimilate and integrate material that they are presented into their thinking patterns and view of life. They often accept new information without question because they have not yet acquired the critical thinking skills of an adult.

Exposure to various forms of disbelief and polytheism is the most perilous aspect of having too many friends that are not Muslims. When one begins to analyze the material available to children, it becomes clear that much of it includes outright polytheism, while others have more hidden forms of disbelief and polytheism.

When children are exposed to these ideas on a constant basis, they begin to believe that they can rely upon other forces or beings to get what they want in life, that there are forces as powerful as Allah, or that there is no God. In many ways, a form of worship of these beings or forces takes place, especially in connection with the materialistic aspect.

{And keep yourself patient [by being] with those who call upon their Lord in the morning and the evening, seeking His countenance. And let not your eyes pass beyond them, desiring adornments of the worldly life, and do not obey one whose heart We have made heedless of Our remembrance and who follows his desire and whose affair is ever [in] neglect.}

(Qur'an 18: 28)

Chapter Fifteen:

The Peer Environment

The Role of Peers

Between the ages of six and twelve, children typically spend approximately 40 percent of their waking hours in the company of peers—children of their own age and status. This is twice the amount of time they spent with peers during the preschool years, and it is accompanied by a corresponding decrease in time spent with parents. As children enter adolescence, peer interaction increases even more. On the average, teenagers spend twice as much time with their peers outside of school as they do with their parents or other adults. This is part of the natural, social transition into adulthood.

Related to the amount of time spent with peers is the influence that peers have on a child or adolescent. This influence functions in many ways, and it is commonly termed 'peer pressure'. Children and teens may feel pressured by their peers to think and act in similar ways. By the teenage years, they may be more concerned about the opinion of friends than that of parents or elders. This social influence is a mutual process. Children and adolescents are not only influenced by their peers, but at the same time influence them as well. They also tend to choose friends who are like themselves. The good news is that most adolescents report that they are more likely to go along with peer pressure that is pro-social than with pressure to misbehave.

The increasing time spent with peers alters parent-child relations. As the parenting role begins to diminish, the influence of peers becomes more significant. However, while the influence of parents decreases, most adolescents continue to share their parents' values. Parents also continue to exert an important influence on their children's development throughout adolescence.

Choosing Righteous Friends

Parents should make every effort to help their children develop friendships with sincere and righteous Muslim peers. Friends should be chosen who believe in and abide by the principles of

Islam and who give proper respect to what Allah and Prophet Muhammad (bpuh) have ordered. They should avoid those peers that are not well-mannered or do not give due attention to their religion and to what pleases or displeases Allah. The Prophet (bpuh) said:

«A person inevitably follows the faith of his friends; therefore, be careful in choosing your friends.» (A reliable hadith narrated by Abu Dâwood and at-Tirmidhi)

The Prophet (bpuh) warned that care should be taken in choosing friends and peer groups, since they will have a strong influence on the individual and his or her character. This is precisely what social and psychological research has discovered, as discussed above. This is important, since befriending righteous and virtuous Muslims is an essential means for staying on the straight path.

In another hadith, Prophet Muhammad (bpuh) said:

«The analogy of a good companion and a bad companion is like that of the seller of musk, and the one who blows the blacksmith's bellows. As for the seller of musk, either he will grant you some, or you buy some from him, or at least you enjoy a pleasant smell from him. As for the one who blows the blacksmith's bellows, either he will burn your clothes or you will get an offensive smell from him.» (Bukhari and Muslim)

In this hadith, the Prophet (bpuh) compared a good companion to a seller of musk and alluded to the virtue of having companions who are good and who have gracious manners, piety, and knowledge. Those types of friends will confer upon others their virtuous ways. Keeping good company with those who are pious results in the attainment of beneficial knowledge, good manners, and righteous actions. The Prophet (bpuh) also forbade us to sit with those who do evil and commit many sins, and likened them to one who blows the blacksmith's bellows. Keeping company with the wicked prevents one from gaining knowledge, good manners, and righteous actions. At times, a Muslim is encouraged by his or her friends to do wrong and to forget his or her duties. S/he may, for example, feel ashamed to leave his or her friends to perform ablution and prayer. In this way, his or her friends cause him or her to deviate from the straight path.

On the Day of Resurrection, the disbelievers will regret having taken evil ones as friends. Allah has described in the Qur'an:

{And the Day the wrongdoer will bite on his hands [in regret] and he will say: Oh, I wish I had taken with the Messenger a way. Oh, woe to me! I wish I had not taken that one [the person who misguided him] as a friend. He led me away from the remembrance after it had come to me. And ever is Satan, to people, a deserter.} (Qur'an 25: 27-29)

In contrast, on that day, the believers will be given the glad tidings of admittance into heaven, along with those who were their righteous companions. Allah has also indicated:

{Close friends, that day, will be enemies to each other, except for the righteous [to whom Allah will say:] O My servants, no fear will there be concerning you this day, nor will you grieve—[you] who believed in Our verses and were Muslims. Enter paradise, you and your kind [those like you], delighted.}

(Qur'an 43: 67-70)

Here is a story on the authority of 'Ali ibn Abi Ṭâlib (May Allah be pleased with him) which says:

[A]ny friendship for other than Allah is turned into enmity, except what was in it for Allah the Mighty and Majestic: Two who are friends for Allah's sake. One of them dies and is given good news that he will be granted paradise, so he remembered his friend and he supplicated for him, saying: O Allah, my friend used to command me to obey You and to obey Your Prophet (bpuh) and used to command me to do good and to forbid me from doing evil. And he told me that I will meet You. O Allah, do not let him go astray after me, until you show him what you have just shown me, until You are satisfied with him, just like You are satisfied with me. So he is told: Had you known what is (written) for your friend, would you have laughed a lot and cried a little. Then his friend dies and their souls are gathered, and both are asked to express their opinions about each other. So each one of them says to his friend: You were the best brother, the best companion and the best friend. And when one of the two disbelieving friends dies, and he is given tidings of hellfire, he remembered his friend and he said: O Allah, my friend used to order me to disobey You and disobey Your Prophet (bpuh), and commanded me to do evil, and forbade me from doing good, and told me that I would not meet You. O Allah, do not guide him after me, until you show him what you have just shown me and until you are dissatisfied with him just like You are dissatisfied with me. Then the other disbelieving friend dies, and their souls are gathered, and both are asked to give their opinions about each other. So each one says to his friend: You were the worst brother, the worst companion and the worst friend.[62]

The benefits of mixing with the righteous are immense, and they will be even more obvious in the hereafter. It is from Allah's blessings upon a child or youth who submits and turns to Allah in worship that s/he is given a brother or sister similar to him or her; thus they are able to encourage each other in their obedience to Allah and adherence to the Sunnah.

Others who take a youth away from remembering Allah and from obeying Him and His Prophet (bpuh), those who fail to remind him or her of his or her daily prayers and those who do not give him or her sincere advice in regard to his or her way of life, are actually foes and not friends.

From a young age, parents should expose their children to others who are righteous by taking them to the mosque, sending them to an Islamic school, and involving them in activities in the Muslim community. In these ways they will have opportunities to develop friendships based upon righteousness. They will also see other children and families worshipping Allah, which will strengthen their own desire to worship.

As parents assist their children in choosing righteous friends, it may be helpful to keep in mind the following questions:

1. Will they assist our child in achieving the purpose for which s/he was brought to life (that is, to worship of Allah) or will they take him or her away from it?

2. Will they desire for our child Allah's pleasure or is that not their concern at all?

3. Will they lead our child closer to paradise or to the hellfire?

Friendship Based upon Love of Allah

The Prophet (bpuh) said:

«Whoever possesses the following three qualities will taste the sweetness of eemân: one to whom Allah and His Messenger become dearer than anything else, one who loves his brother (or sister) solely for Allah's sake, and one who hates to revert to disbelief just as he hates to be thrown into the fire.» (Bukhari and Muslim)

Friendship in Islam is based upon mutual love and respect. This is one of the ways through which a person may taste the sweetness of eemân. When a Muslim befriends and loves his or her brother or sister in Islam, s/he loves him or her for the sake of Allah. This means that his or her love for that brother or sister is connected to his or her love for Allah.

S/he loves him or her and treats him or her in the manner that Allah has ordained. S/he loves him or her because they share a special bond that can never be broken, the bond of faith in Allah, the Creator of all humankind. It is a bond between hearts and minds that brings them close in a unique and special way; so much so that they are willing to sacrifice anything for each other knowing they will gain the pleasure of Allah in the process. Nothing between them is ever done for worldly gain or purpose.

The Messenger of Allah said:

«On the Day of Judgement, Allah, the Most High, will announce: Where are those persons who love each other for the sake of My pleasure? This day I am going to shelter them in the shade provided by Me. Today there is no shade except My shade.» (Muslim)

Brothers and sisters in Islam who love each other for Allah's sake will find His shade on the day when there will be no other shade. The rewards that Allah gives for this love are beyond our imagination and beyond what we are capable of earning. This emphasizes the importance of loving each other for the sake of Allah.

In another story:

«A man went to visit a brother of his in another village. Allah sent an angel to wait for him on the road. When the man came along the angel asked him: Where are you headed?

He replied: I am going to visit a brother of mine who lives in this village.

The angel asked: Have you done him any favour (for which you are now seeking repayment)?

He said: No, I just love him for the sake of Allah.

The angel told him: I am a messenger to you from Allah, sent to tell you that He loves you as you love your brother for His sake.» (Muslim)

The significance of this cannot be overstated when we understand that our love for a brother or sister in Islam brings us Allah's love.

At the level of eemân, to develop a friendship for Allah's sake means to establish relationships of love and trust for His sake. This entails assistance, alliance, and loyalty. Loyalty for the sake of Allah really means to come to the assistance of those who are obedient to Him, even if it requires immense sacrifices. It requires us to ally ourselves for the sake of Allah, and it requires us to ally ourselves to Muslims wherever we find them. This brotherhood and sisterhood transcends all worldly barriers such as culture, race, language, and socioeconomic status. There is no better friendship than friendship for the sake of Allah.

Chapter Sixteen:
The Community Environment

{And indeed this, your religion [Ummah][63] is one religion [Ummah], and I am your Lord, so fear Me.}

(Qur'an 23: 52)

    A community is basically a group of people having common interests, goals, principles, and rights. The main element of sharing something in common defines a community. However, it goes beyond that, and for the Muslim community it is a much deeper experience. To be effective, a community needs to be organized, cohesive, cooperative, and active. A true Muslim community will have all of those things in addition to being the carrier of Islam, the Qur'an and the Sunnah of the Prophet (bpuh). Allah has mentioned:

{And thus We have made you a median [just]) community that you will be witnesses over the people and the Messenger will be a witness over you...}

(Qur'an 2: 143)

    As the standard bearers of Islam, we are examples for all people, and in particular, for the next generation. This is the responsibility of the community and it is a responsibility that needs to be taken seriously. When we fail to practice Islam or to bring up our children as Muslims, we not only harm ourselves and our family, but we also negatively impact the whole community.

    In relation to nurturing eemân and developing an Islamic personality, the youth learn values, morals, attitudes, and ideals not only from individual people, but they also acquire them from reference groups. These are social groups to which a person belongs and with which common aspects are shared. For a Muslim youth, the most important reference group should be the Muslim community. For that to happen, the Muslim community needs to be available. Youth need to be encouraged to participate and made to feel that they are important members of the community who have something to contribute. If these elements are not present, the youth will turn to other readily available options.

Encourage a Sense of Belonging to the Muslim Nation

Children should be taught the importance of brotherhood and sisterhood between Muslims and a sense of belonging to the Muslim community. They should read and know about Muslims in other lands who are suffering and need our care and assistance. This hadith of the Prophet (bpuh) should be in their minds:

«You see the believers in their mutual love, kindness and compassion are like the human body, in that when one of its parts is in agony the entire body feels the pain, and experiences sleeplessness and fever.» (Bukhari and Muslim)

As part of one body, we should feel joy when other Muslims are joyous and sadness when others are sad. Youth should be trained to do the best that they can to achieve the goals of the community and to develop solutions to the multitude of problems that face it. They need to understand that as responsible members of the community, these problems are not distant or remote, but rather their own concerns as well.

Practical Suggestions for Developing a Sense of Community

Children and youth should be taken to the mosque or to social gatherings on a regular basis where they have the opportunity to interact with other Muslim children. This is particularly true for families living in non-Muslim countries. Beginning around the age of six or seven, they can be taken to gatherings to sit with grown-ups. This will help to increase their understanding and wisdom. They will also naturally try to imitate adults, so appropriate adult role models should be provided. The Companions used to bring their children with them when they sat with the Prophet (bpuh). For example, Mu'âwiyah ibn Qurrah narrated (from his father), that:

«The Prophet (bpuh) used to sit with a group of his Companions. One man had his little son with him; he would bring him from behind and make him sit in front of him...» (A sound hadith narrated by an-Nasâ'i)

Young boys should be introduced to congregational prayer in the mosque—including funeral prayers. Eid prayers should be attended by the whole family, and special activities should be planned in the community on these occasions. The community should break the fast and celebrate the Eid together.

Programs and services need to be available for youth so that they obtain a sense of belonging. If no programs are available, they need to be developed to suit various age ranges and interests. This may include such things as religious study groups, Qur'an memorization, extra-curricular activities, sports activities, and so on. The main idea is to develop activities and an environment in which Muslim youth can interact and develop the bonds of community.

It is through these efforts that an environment of brotherhood and social responsibility will develop. Members of the community will support each other, help each other in need, and offer useful advice. This will add to the mutual love among the Muslims and enhance the eemân of each individual member of the community.

Conclusion

The beliefs that an individual carries with him or her throughout his or her lifetime are the most significant aspects of his or her existence, as they are the foundation for all else. They will influence his or her choices, behaviour, social interactions, emotions and ultimately his destined place in the hereafter. If a person was a disbeliever all of his or her life and then accepted Islam near the end of that life, s/he would be counted amongst the people of paradise (with the grace of Allah). If another person performed many good deeds during his or her lifetime but died a disbeliever, that person's deeds would not benefit him or her in the least. These scenarios highlight the importance of belief in the Islamic framework.

It was for this reason that the Prophet taught his Companions the principles of aqeedah for 13 years before introducing the practical aspects of the religion. He wanted to ensure that firm eemân and commitment to Islam were built into their hearts, that they were prepared to face the challenges that lie ahead of them, and that they would be willing to defend Islam with their wealth and their lives. A sign of true faith is the willingness to give up everything in this worldly life for the sake of Allah and for Islamic principles and values.

As discussed in the preceding text, the Islamic belief system is built upon the pillars of eemân: belief in Allah, His angels, His prophets, His books, the Day of Judgement and the hereafter, and divine will and predestination. As Muslim parents, it is our duty to instil these beliefs in the hearts and minds of our children by connecting them in various ways to the pillars of faith throughout our daily lives and interactions. Their relationship with Allah should be the most important one in their lives and they should consistently be aware that Allah is aware of their every thought, feeling and deed. This insight will give them the ability to discern right from wrong and to always choose that which is most pleasing to Allah. Lawful choices will be made regardless of the pressures, temptations, or sacrifices they may face.

We should continually recall that parenting is a serious responsibility. What we do and the choices we make will affect our children for the rest of their lives (in this world and the hereafter). We should provide the proper environment and nourishment that are required for eemân to mature and flourish. Then, inshallah, we can watch as our children grow to become obedient servants of Allah, develop Islamic personalities and identities, and represent Islam as it should be represented.

By Allah's grace, you will reap the rewards of your efforts and hard work as you see your children blossom and flower. Your children will appreciate the gift that you have given to them, you will feel a sense of accomplishment, and the community will be strengthened and activated. The rewards waiting in the hereafter (inshallah) will be even greater.

Notes

1 *taqwâ*: fearful awareness of Allah; being mindful of Allah; pious dedication; being careful not to transgress the bounds set by Allah.

2 Wherever possible, Arabic terms have been translated into English. In cases where we have chosen to retain the Arabic, the transliterated word or phrase is shown in italics the first time it appears in the text; the term is also defined in the Glossary found at the end of this book. (Editor)

3 In this Preface, the author is quoting translated meanings of several well-known verses of the Qur'an. (Editor)

4 *zakât*: obligatory charity: an 'alms tax' on wealth payable by Muslims and to be distributed to other Muslims who qualify as recipients.

5 *tawḥeed*: (belief in) the Oneness of Allah: that He alone deserves to be worshipped and that He has no partners.

6 al-Ashqar, *Belief in Allah*, 29-31.

7 The translations of the meanings of the verses of the Qur'an in this book have been taken [with some changes to the text to clarify meaning] from Saheeh International, *The Qur'an: Arabic Text with Corresponding English Meanings*.

8 Hadith: the collected sayings and actions of Prophet Muhammad (bpuh) that with the Qur'an form the basis of Islamic law.

9 al-Ashqar, *Belief in Allah*, 34.

10 al-Ashqar, *Belief in Allah*, 35.

11 al-Ashqar, *Belief in Allah*, 39-40.

12 hadith: a saying or action of Prophet Muhammad (bpuh) that was remembered and recorded by his Companions and followers.

13 Angel Gabriel (or *Jibreel* in Arabic): the archangel who transmitted the verses of the Qur'an and other communication from Allah to Prophet Muhammad (bpuh). (Editor)

14 Ibn al-Qayyim, *al-Fawâ'id*, 107. Translation quoted in Zarabozo, *He Came to Teach You Your Religion*, 86.

15 Zarabozo, *He Came to Teach You Your Religion*, 86.

16 Zarabozo, *He Came to Teach You Your Religion*, 87.

17 Zarabozo, *He Came to Teach You Your Religion*, 89.

18 Zarabozo, *He Came to Teach You Your Religion*, 90-91.

19 Zarabozo, *He Came to Teach You Your Religion*, 91.

20 Zarabozo, *He Came to Teach You Your Religion*, 94-95.

21 Zarabozo, *He Came to Teach You Your Religion*, 198.

22 Zarabozo, *He Came to Teach You Your Religion*, 198-199.

23 *Fitnah* also has other meanings that are more negative such as persecution, *shirk* (associating partners with Allah) and disbelief, falling into sin, confusing truth with falsehood, and so on. For our purposes, we will only be using it in the sense of 'trial' or 'test'.

24 'Adoption' here refers to the practice of changing the child's family name to match the name of the family in which s/he is to be raised and erasing all evidence that the child has his or her own biological heritage, and should not be taken to mean that Islam forbids families to bring orphans up with the same love and treatment that they accord their own biological children. On the contrary, according to a sound hadith, raising an orphan in kindness and equity is considered to be a highly praiseworthy act, whose reward is paradise. To that end, the advice in this book should be taken to heart by foster parents as well. (Editor)

25 dirhams and dinars: originally, silver and gold coins; both are also contemporary units of currency in some countries.

26 *Sunnah*: the practice and collected sayings of Prophet Muhammad (bpuh) that together with the Qur'an forms the basis of Islamic law.

27 Shaykh al-Islam: An honorary title meaning 'Scholar of Islam'. (Editor)

28 Ibn Taymiyah, *The Necessity of the Straight Path*, 1:470, quoted in Al-Baatilee, "Learning Arabic is a Fard (Obligation) on Every Muslim," *Islamicweb.com*, http://www.islamicnetwork.com/index.php/weblog/comments/learning_arabic_in_an_obligation_fard_on_every_muslim (accessed December 14, 2008).

29 A useful resource on this topic is al-Munajjid, *The Prophet's Methods of Correcting People's Mistakes*. (Editor)

30 *jinn*: unseen creatures created from smokeless fire; see Glossary for additional explanation.

31 The translation of the meaning of this verse is from Abdullah Yusuf Ali. (Editor)

32 al-Ashqar, *The World of the Noble Angels*, 58-59.

33 al-Ashqar, *The World of the Noble Angels*, 66-67.

34 al-Ashqar, *The World of the Noble Angels*, 80-83.

35 The Night of Decree (or Night of Power), or *Laylat al-Qadr* in Arabic, is one of the last ten nights of the month of Ramadan. Worship and other forms of good deeds performed on this night are rewarded as if one had been performing them for a thousand months.

36 Descendants: The twelve tribes of Israel descended from Jacob.

37 From *Zâd al-Ma'âd* by Ibn al-Qayyim al-Jawziyah, summarized in al-Ashqar, *The Messengers and the Messages in the Light of the Qur'an and Sunnah*, 55-56.

38 *soorah* or *soorat*: chapter of the Qur'an.

39 The Preserved Slate, called *al-Lawḥ al-Mahfoodh* in Arabic, is the writing tablet in heaven on which Allah's words and decrees are engraved for all eternity. (Editor)

40 al-Ashqar, *Divine Will and Predestination*, 21-23.

41 «It is reported on the authority of 'Ubâdah ibn as-Sâmit that he said to his son: O son! You will never taste true faith until you know that whatever afflicts you would not have missed you, and whatever has missed you would never have come to you. I heard the Messenger of Allah (bpuh) say: The first thing Allah created was the pen; He commanded it to write. It said: My Lord, what shall I write? He (the Exalted) said: Write down what has been ordained for all things until the

establishment of the Hour. O my son! I heard Allah's Messenger say: Whoever dies believing something other than this does not belong to me.» (A sound hadith recorded by Abu Dâwood)

In another narration by Imam Aḥmad, it was reported:

«Verily, the first thing which Allah Most High created was the pen, and He said to it: Write; and in that very hour all what was to occur (was written) - up to the Day of Resurrection.» (A sound hadith recorded by Ahmad)

In another version from Ibn Wahb, it was said: Allah's Messenger (bpuh) said: «Whoever disbelieved in destiny, the good and the bad of it, will be burnt in the fire of hell.» (A sound hadith narrated by at-Tabarâni)

42 *Aqeedat al-Isfarâ'eeni* as quoted in al-Ashqar, *Divine Will and Predestination*, 33.

43 al-Ashqar, *Divine Will and Predestination*, 33.

44 al-Ashqar, *Divine Will and Predestination*, 37.

45 *Majmoo' al-Fatâwâ li Shaykh al-Islâm* as quoted in al-Ashqar, *Divine Will and Predestination*, 25.

46 Translated as above in Ibrahim and Johnson-Davies, *An-Nawawi's Forty Hadith*, hadith no. 19.

47 Translated as above in Ibrahim and Johnson-Davies, *An-Nawawi's Forty Hadith*, hadith no. 19.

48 Quoted in Muslim Student Association, University of Southern California, *Compendium of Muslim Texts: Biographies of the Sahabah*, http://www.usc.edu/dept/MSA/history/biographies/sahaabah/bio.ABDULLAH_IBN_ABBAS.html (accessed December, 2008).

49 From *Companions around the Prophet*

50 Imam Bukhari and Imam Muslim.

51 From *Companions around the Prophet*

52 From *Companions around the Prophet*.

53 From *Companions around the Prophet*

54 See the full hadith cited below.

55 *mâ shâ' Allâh*: *lit.* '[It is] what Allah wanted'; an expression of appreciation for something someone has done.

56 The reason the Prophet (bpuh) asked the boy his permission is that in Islamic etiquette, one serves others starting with those on one's right, and goes around the 'circle' until those on the left are served. The boy thus had the right to be served first. (Editor)

57 *tasleem(ah)*: the act of saying *as-salâmu 'alaykum wa raḥmat Allâh* to end the prayer.

58 *witr*: *lit.* an odd number: a single unit of supererogatory prayer, to be prayed any time after the evening (*'ishâ'*) prayer and before the call for the dawn prayer.

59 Abu Dâwood, mentioned in al-Qahtani, *Fortress of the Muslim*, 19.

60 Eid: *lit.* festival; the two celebrations: one at the end of Ramadan and the other at the culmination of the Hajj.

61 Fatwa of the Standing Committee for Issuing Fatwas, "Ruling on building toilets that face the qiblah," *Islam-qa.com*, http://www.islamqa.com/en/ref/69808 (accessed December, 2008).

62 Ibn Katheer, *Tafsir Ibn Kathir*, vol. 8.

63 Ummah: community or nation: *usu.* used to refer to the entire global community of Muslims.

www.ingramcontent.com/pod-product-compliance
Lightning Source LLC
Chambersburg PA
CBHW072159070526
44585CB00015B/1218